T0110011

Negotiating in the Real World

GETTING THE DEAL YOU WANT

Victor Gotbaum

A Fireside Book
Published by Simon & Schuster
New York   London   Toronto   Sydney   Singapore

FIRESIDE
Rockefeller Center
1230 Avenue of the Americas
New York, NY 10020

First Fireside Edition 2000
FIRESIDE and colophon are registered trademarks
of Simon & Schuster, Inc.

Designed by Pagesetters

Manufactured in the United States of America

10 9 8 7 6 5 4 3 2 1

The Library of Congress has cataloged the Simon & Schuster edition as follows:
Gotbaum, Victor.
    Negotiating in the real world: getting the deal you want/ Victor Gotbaum.
      pp.   cm.
    Includes index.
    1. Negotiation in business. 2. Communication in management.
  I. Title.
  HD58.6.G666   1999
  658.4´052—dc21   98-50658 CIP

ISBN 0-684-81543-5
    0-684-86555-6 (Pbk)

ACKNOWLEDGMENTS

Whenever anyone recommended that I write a book, I typically responded, "I'm a talker, not a writer." Nevertheless, some friends persisted, insisting that as a labor leader I had something to say and should make the effort. Among this group of cheerleaders were Alexandra Penney, Molly O'Neill, and Arthur Samuelson. I ignored their positive assertions, knowing that while they were all talented writers, I was not. My wife, Betsy, was uncharacteristically silent on the matter, but it soon became apparent that she too thought it was a good idea.

One evening during a dinner party, Betsy had a private conversation with Lynn Nesbit, one of New York's most successful literary agents. After dinner, Lynn approached me and told me Betsy had indicated I wanted to write a book. Before I had a chance to deny it, I found myself scheduled for drinks with her to discuss the prospect. The woman is a pro. She started negotiations with a foregone conclusion: I would write a book.

While writing can be a lonely process, assistance would be forthcoming. Simon & Schuster provided me with an excellent soft-sell editor, Bob Bender, and several friends, including Jerry Schoenfeld and Oscar de la Renta, willingly shared their own negotiating experiences for use in the book. For over forty years, Saki Meyashiro was my executive assistant. She would never admit it, but she delayed her retirement until the word processing for this manuscript was complete.

My most important assistance came from a colleague and friend, Rose Diamond. Rose organized and edited the book or, as Betsy says, "translated it into English." She has the incredible facility of making me sound coherent.

To Betsy Gotbaum

CONTENTS

PART ONE

The Basics of Negotiating

Introduction

Negotiating is a face-to-face human drama that can be as genteel as croquet or as brutal as a prizefight. Like these sports, negotiating depends on the talent, experience, and physical and emotional condition of the opponents. Some people are great at negotiating. Others tremble at the very idea. Yet nearly everybody must negotiate. You buy a house, sign an employment contract, get a divorce. Whether you're a mother working out the details of your baby-sitter's wages and hours or a corporate executive entering into a major merger, sooner or later you will find yourself at the bargaining table. So what's a mother or mogul to do?

This book explores some vital principles of negotiating that you can use in every aspect of your life. It will also help you to appreciate the importance of negotiations in events that range from labor-management discussions to peace treaties among nations.

There is no exact how-to formula, but following certain principles can make you a better negotiator. Whether the negotiations are formal or informal, professional or personal, the same principles apply. Your preparation for negotiations depends on assessing and evaluating the overall and specific context of the talks, and your own and your adversary's personality, power, position, strengths and weaknesses, and negotiating style. You must also determine the appropriate role you should play in the talks and when and how to seek the support of others.

One of the most important ingredients in becoming a better negotiator is experience, which is not always easy to come by. Although there is no substitute for firsthand experience, the examples in this book will fill the gap and enable you to do what you will need to do most during negotiations: think on your feet. This understanding will dictate your strategy. It may even cause you to decide that you should not lead the negotiations, but rather should participate in them in a different way.

The principles and the examples I use to support them are based on my experiences as a labor leader and consultant over the past forty years, as well as my experiences as a husband, father, grandfather, worker, ex-husband, friend, consumer, client, and patient.

From the beginning of my career as a labor leader, what I loved most were the negotiations. In keeping with my own principles, I begin this book in the same way that I propose you begin your preparation for negotiations—by describing my own background and the environment that led to the writing of this book. In negotiations, and in learning to negotiate, you will need to know who you are dealing with. So, about me . . .

•   •   •

Papa was a loser. Although he was intelligent, he could not stay with a job, could not build a future, and kept his family poor. Consequently, my older brother, Irv, and I entered the world of work at a very young age. At age thirteen, I held a full-time (fifty-hour-per-week) job, washing dishes and making sandwiches, for weekly wages of six dollars. (This was between 1935 and 1938).

Like Irv, I was tired all the time. Irv was not only working, he was attending college. Unlike Irv, I was truant . . . most of the time. Thanks to Irv, I managed to receive a high school diploma from Brooklyn's Samuel Tilden High School. In retrospect, his appeals to my teachers and guidance counselors to allow me to take final exams in classes I had rarely attended were classic negotiations. Brother Irv, however, did not negotiate with me. He insisted I study; he made sure I would pass the exams.

After high school graduation and military service, I married and went to college on the GI Bill, working part time and seasonally at Unity House, the International Ladies Garment Workers Union rest camp. There I saw firsthand the activities of many labor leaders.

When I completed my master's degree at Columbia University's School of International Affairs, I went to work in the Bureau of International Labor Affairs, where I did domestic programming for foreign trade union visitors. I felt, however, that if I really wanted to stay in international labor, I would need to do some overseas work. I was fortunate to be tapped to join a team charged with setting up a first-of-its-kind labor education program in Turkey.

I returned from Turkey with a hunger for a more basic knowledge about the American labor movement and labor itself. I accepted a job with the Amalgamated Meat Cutters as an assistant director of education and found this to be more satisfying than working in international labor. In 1957, after being fired by the director of education because of a personality conflict, I was soon hired by Arnold Zander, the head of the American Federation of State, County and Municipal Employees (AFSCME), a man who loved international affairs. He was impressed by my background and asked me to take over the Chicago local. This operation was almost nonexistent, with just fragments of union organization and little cohesiveness, but it provided me with my first real hands-on experience in running a union. I had observed negotiations and participated in strikes with the Meat Cutters, but this was the real thing. The work with AFSCME afforded me not only participation, but a leadership position. Sadly, it was leadership without power. Mayor Richard Daley's authoritarianism made sure of that. However, although being an adversary to Daley was difficult and depressing, the work in Chicago gave me valuable experience.

At the University of Chicago Lying-In Hospital, I did my first negotiations. Management was offering a four-cent hourly wage increase, and I was trying to increase it to five cents. The nickel was important since it would have been the largest raise ever achieved for the hospital workers. When management came around from four to five cents, it was a major triumph. One cent an hour made me a hero with the negotiating committee and the members of the hospital local. It solidified my position.

This victory had very little to do with material gain. The penny was of small importance. The significance was in my demonstration to the local union leadership that I could meet management as an equal and leave the bargaining table in a stronger position. I was a paid professional. It was imperative that I prove my worth.

I stayed with AFSCME more than thirty-two years, and negotiating became my life's work. I now look back and realize Chicago couldn't have been a better experience. There's nothing quite like getting some bruises when you're a young man. It hurts, but it makes you think.

Several years later, in the sixties, a group of us formed a palace revolution against Arnold Zander, AFSCME's president. We believed, and I still believe, that he was a wonderful civil service reformer but was inadequate as a labor leader.

We wanted more militancy for the union, more activism in terms of obtaining collective bargaining rights and accelerated organizing. In other words, we wanted dramatic change. The change came about when we elected as president Jerry Wurf, the head of the New York City District Council, the largest in our union and the most sophisticated. Jerry's election was a double plus for me. He moved to Washington as the president of AFSCME, replacing Zander, and I replaced him as the head of the New York City District Council, the second most important position in the AFSCME union at the time. I was also put in charge of international affairs for the entire union. With New York as my major base and with the international affairs activity, I was now in a broad and rewarding arena.

Personally, a bad marriage was becoming worse. When I accepted the New York City job, my wife, Sarah, refused to relocate from Evanston, Illinois, leaving the children disturbed and me angry. She finally came east after a year. This was the first major sign of a breakup that would occur more than a decade later, when I met and fell in love with my wife, Betsy.

The divorce was long, drawn out, and tortured and was probably the most unsuccessful and unrewarding negotiation of my life. I describe it later in the book to demonstrate what can happen when the basic principles of negotiating are undermined by emotion. This is a common pitfall, particularly in personal or everyday negotiations: real estate transactions, job situations, and so forth. Emotional involvement can undermine *every* type of negotiation. But with personal and everyday negotiations the fact that you are both negotiator and client makes objectivity an even greater challenge. This certainly was the case with my divorce.

The union I headed in New York City, District Council 37, became the largest urban union in the country, growing from 25,000 to its current membership of 125,000. The union's goal was to develop the full potential of the members—to go beyond the job experience. We would assure the members of benefits no other trade unionists enjoyed. We established the first college at a union headquarters and a legal resources unit of some fifty lawyers that protected workers off the job as well as on the job. The workers participated in the union's activities. We built an effective political machine that gave me a leading role in city, state, and national politics.

In my personal life, despite a difficult marriage or maybe because of it, Sarah and I had four wonderful children. My kids have given me numerous opportunities to hone my negotiating skills. I can't remember a time when I wasn't negotiating something with at least one of them.

Whether personal or professional, I loved and still love negotiating. Professionally, I don't just mean the multimillion-dollar, sometimes billion-dollar, contracts. I also loved negotiating workers' grievances—grievances involving workers' being unfairly discharged, discriminated against, or otherwise demeaned. Few people realize that a union can spend up to 60 or 70 percent of its time on grievance negotiations—protecting workers on the job.

But the mother of all negotiations were those that took place during the New York City fiscal crisis in the mid-1970s. The crisis was a major change in the life of New York City, the unions, and myself. This was a fiscal crisis, and finances were my weak point, so the crisis made for an incredible challenge. The whole world seemed to be standing on its head, and somehow the City had to come out of it. I knew we would.

Assisting in this was my introduction to Felix Rohatyn. He was an investment banker for Lazard Frères and had the confidence of Governor Carey. After an initial bit of suspicion, I trusted him. He wanted a positive solution, and he wanted the unions to share in that solution. We kept our eyes on the same ball: a solvent New York City without giving up the city's autonomy to the state or federal government.

A militant friend asked me what made for the major change in my approach during the fiscal crisis. I said, "survival." We didn't have the luxury of procrastinating. We had to work together. Felix Rohatyn, my wife, Betsy, the bankers, and the corporate world helped in that change. I believed, and still believe, that the experience changed many of the participants, including me. We went from an antagonistic and adversarial position to one of compromise and agreement through negotiations. The union and its members sacrificed much more than the other stakeholders, but we had much more to lose.

In 1987 I retired after thirty-two years with AFSCME. I believed that both the institution and I needed a change. In addition, I had been critical of labor leaders who held on too long.

It was also my loss of energy at the bargaining table that signaled a need for change. I could no longer go around the clock, negotiating for twenty-four-hour stretches without growing tired. The most difficult aspect of the job was my intolerance of my associates. I had to pay attention to the danger signs.

There is nothing compared to the give and take at the bargaining table. I loved it, and—I say it with my usual lack of humility—I was good at it. And that's why, after I stepped down, I was willing to write a book about it.

When I began the book, I did a great deal of reading on negotiations, but my experiences seemed far more valuable than my reading. Most popular and commercially successful books were far too academic and theoretical for me. Too many of their examples came from a hypothetical world, not from the actual world. Some of the examples and principles were excellent, but I wanted to write a book that based its principles on actual experience, a book where the world, including the adversaries, is very real. The books I read on negotiations to prepare for writing this book make negotiations sound too easy. They claim that almost anybody can be a good negotiator. I disagree. There are people who don't want to negotiate. There are people who *should* not negotiate. Certain negotiations demand a kind of personality that some people do not have. Other types of negotiations require professionalism.

Everyone will be involved in negotiations at some time, but that doesn't make them negotiators. No one who is uncomfortable taking on that responsibility should negotiate. Participation in negotiations is important, but this does not mean that you must negotiate. You may be better suited to acting as chief adviser to your negotiator. My wife, Betsy, knows more about the economics of buying a house than I do—but she refuses to do the actual negotiating since she considers it bargaining. My close friend Ralph Pepe, an expert on real estate and taxes, turns the financial information over to me. He insists that I do the negotiating.

Even in the most personal negotiations—an argument between husband and wife, a divorce, or the purchase of a house—negotiations are never really one-on-one. There are always others involved: the children in a divorce or the purchase of a house, the spouse in negotiating a large purchase or resolving a marital dispute, the outsiders you bring into an argument. Outside representation of the parties takes place not only in major collective bargaining and in business mergers; it can also take place in what may appear on the surface to be a disagreement between just two people.

Adversaries can be dogmatic about issues, goals, and policies. It is important, however, not to be dogmatic about how to arrive at solutions. There may be different roads to take. The academic ex-

perts sometimes dwell in an ideal world where the adversaries become manageable and have to live together after the situation is
resolved. This is not necessarily so; generally, however, regardless
of anger or policy difficulties, in most negotiations you must keep
in mind that you have to work with your adversary after the storm
subsides. New York's mayor Ed Koch and I could tear each other
apart, but we both knew that in many areas we would have to
work together—lobbying the state legislature in Albany, for example. We never allowed our anger to make us forget an important
fact. He was the mayor of the city, and I headed the largest union.
It helped neither one of us to allow the other to bleed to death.

Almost by definition, negotiations require face-to-face interac-
tion between individuals. There is incredible variation in terms of
the personalities who are adversaries, and you react in different
ways to different people. Mayor Ed Koch was not Mayor Abe
Beame, and my strategies in negotiating with them varied, although the results may have been the same.

Most books on negotiations advise you to turn the other cheek
and to dissipate a harsh, offensive attack with a kind, gentle, and
principled retort. Under certain circumstances and for personal
reasons, this may make sense, but it can also be counterproductive. I could do it with Abe Beame, but it would have been pure
folly with Ed Koch.

It is not necessary to avoid confrontation in negotiations. It is
not necessary to love thy adversary. You don't have to account for
the fact that there will always be a tomorrow. In fact, confrontation and the anger that you bring to negotiations can be very appropriate and very positive.

My personality doesn't allow for constant lovableness. I can be
humorous, and I can be sensitive, but mainly I can be very tough.
Herbert Haber, chief negotiator for Mayor John Lindsay, paid me a
supreme compliment when he was quoted in *The New York Times:*
"Vic will cut your heart out if he feels you are hurting his members." Mayor Koch and I could work ourselves into a lather during
negotiations yet conclude contracts on a positive note. We negotiated some meaningful and important contracts, yet we always had

a healthy distaste for each other. Negotiations can be bloody and vulgar and still produce a positive outcome.

The role you play in the negotiations will depend on your individual talents and abilities as well as on the size and condition of your ego. If this book gives men and women more know-how and security in choosing their appropriate role and performing it better, more fruitful negotiations will occur, and I—as well as you— will be happy.

Chapter One

EVALUATING YOURSELF AS A NEGOTIATOR

KNOW YOURSELF

Some books on negotiations describe in detail how to act in certain situations, as if there can be a formula response. This form of pat advice is arrant nonsense that can cripple you as a negotiator. You'll devise the formula. You'll react according to your own feelings. In other words, in negotiations, you will be you.

Knowing yourself, understanding your own style and characteristics, your own strengths, weaknesses, and prejudices, and how you typically react to others' styles and idiosyncrasies is key to your success as a negotiator. You may think it is easier to follow some formulaic response, but knowing yourself will be far more productive.

This does not mean that in order to become an effective negotiator you will have to undergo psychoanalysis. It does mean that you will need to take an objective view of yourself, focusing on the elements most critical to and most likely to affect the negotiations. Although I describe individually the major characteristics or attributes that make for a better negotiator, in practice, they relate to each other and are often interdependent.

Authority is the chief attribute a negotiator must possess. It can come from position, intelligence, reputation, or sheer attitude (personality). A weak, vacillating negotiator lacks authority. The only thing worse than not having authority is having it and then losing it.

Power is very much related to authority. When you are holding the cards, you clearly have an important advantage. How you deal with power, whether it's on your side or your adversary's, is as important as possessing it.

Principle is very much in the mind of the beholder. The definition of principle is up to the individual negotiator. The degree to which principle is driving the negotiations, or is at stake in the negotiations, needs to be assessed and understood.

Intellectual ability is not just your own personal wisdom. Knowing what you don't know is as important as knowing what you know. An adviser, friend, or expert can become part of your intellect and knowledge base.

Knowing your limitations is a special kind of knowledge, different from intellectual ability. It can take the form of knowing from the start that overwhelming victory may not be yours and will not be yours without outside help.

Sensitivity is tied to emotion. Your level of sensitivity to the issues and empathy for the players can make the difference between winning or losing. Most important, be understanding of and sympathetic to the problems of those you represent. Selfishness and self-indulgence can have grave consequences. The more aware you are of your allies' needs, the less likely you are to react emotionally or inappropriately for your own benefit. Understanding your own personal prejudices can keep you from becoming too emotionally involved at the expense of those you represent. Blowing your top or becoming paralyzed by your own emotional reactions are common and costly mistakes that you have within your power to avoid.

These personal characteristics define your ability as a negotiator. Ability, however, is variable. Even seasoned negotiators cannot fully predict the outcome in certain negotiations. You must look at yourself as a negotiator in the context of the specific circumstances of *each* negotiation. For a variety of reasons you may be effective in some circumstances but ineffective in others. The best of us sometimes find ourselves on the defensive, which is one of the reasons I devote a chapter to negotiations that fail.

It is also important to understand that you will react differently to different people. We have all encountered people who bring out the best in us; then there are those who push our buttons or grate on our nerves. Whatever the reaction, it is often instinctive—your own chemistry—and the better you understand it, the more freedom you will have to be you.

It's my nature, for example, to be nice, soft, even passive with nice people. And it is my nature to be nasty as all hell with vindictive or negative people, or with people who demean or have large, smothering egos. I don't suffer them gladly, and I react emotionally. This is why I was almost always gentle around Abe Beame and brash and boisterous around Ed Koch.

Self-awareness will make the difference. It will help prevent you from reacting counterproductively. It will help you to control your natural instincts while maintaining your sense of security in dealing with different people and situations. It will also give you a valuable weapon: flexibility.

Each negotiation can bring out a different side of your personality, with the characteristics coming into play as you are challenged. This means you should evaluate your own attributes every time you are involved in a negotiation, for as the dynamics of the situation change, you may need to change or adjust.

It can be difficult to evaluate your own abilities and potential performance as a negotiator objectively. There are those who devalue themselves and those who overestimate themselves. If you cannot overcome a sense of weakness prior to the talks, discuss the situation with a trusted friend, colleague, or professional negotiator. Many attorneys are professional negotiators. You may simply need assurance and security. Or you may need to play a secondary role in the negotiations. An objective opinion can help you determine your role.

AUTHORITY

Of all of the attributes of a good negotiator, your level of authority, going into the talks and during the talks, is key. Authority can come about through personality, position, intelligence, or the right combination of all three.

During the New York City fiscal crisis in the mid-1970s, two men whose authority was largely based on their personalities and intelligence joined forces. The unions' main consultant, Jack Bigel, and the governor's representative, Felix Rohatyn, formed a winning combination.

Jack was the expert on numbers. As my research director, Alan Viani, would say, Jack was the only one who knew the numbers. He also knew the characters in every play, and he knew how to play those characters. He sincerely believed that he was in charge; in fact, he was. This knowledge and attitude gave him authority, and he used it well. He was loyal to his clients and hell on wheels with his adversaries. I was thankful that I was one of his clients.

When I first met Felix Rohatyn, he was the new kid on the block—an unknown entity to all of us. He was sent in by Governor Hugh Carey to represent New York State, to act as a facilitator between the corporations and the unions. Like Jack Bigel, Felix had one of the best minds I've ever encountered. It was priceless during the fiscal crisis. He also didn't allow anybody to take advantage of him.

Felix came into this difficult situation new and untested, but he came in with authority. We had to respect him because he was the governor's representative. But we also felt that we had to test him. He was unflappable. He combined his excellent mind with decisiveness and purpose, and in doing so, his authority grew. We stopped testing him early in the negotiations and began to work with him on a very positive level.

Jack and Felix were incredibly skillful in working with others. Who they were and what they knew commanded respect and allowed them to control, and ultimately resolve, the fiscal crisis. They used their authority very well indeed.

Authority is an element of every type of negotiation. In purchasing a large or small item, or in buying a service, the consumer has the authority, provided the item is not a rare or one-of-a-kind commodity. Your ability to choose puts you in the driver's seat. In family matters, your position within the family and your expertise concerning the specific issue will dictate your level of authority in negotiating with the other family members. On the job, authority is largely based on your status within the organization and your reputation.

Having authority, and knowing you have it, can alter your typical negotiating style. It can give you the ability to manipulate a particular situation or to play it softer than usual. This happened in my dealings with Norman Adler, the union's political consultant. As executive director of the union, by definition I had the authority to make key personnel decisions but chose to play this down in my negotiations with Norman.

The head of my political action department was leaving, and I needed a replacement. Norman, an associate professor at the City University of New York, was available, but not excited about the position. Leaving the security of his position in academia troubled him. I felt it was important that I bring him in. The incentive for Norman was a $10,000 salary increase. Although he did not want to leave his first love, education, he hesitantly accepted the job.

Just as Norman was beginning to get his feet wet at the new job, the directorship of the union's education department became available. Norman zoomed in. This was more his cup of tea, and he wanted it. A very unhappy Norman confronted me when I held out. His arguments were compelling. He was an excellent educator. He had demonstrated this during his brief tenure in the political action department. I also did not want an unhappy Norman. I manipulated the situation and played to Norman's ego, telling him, "Norman, if you can find a replacement to do your job, we'll make the switch. With all my problems, I don't want to take care of education and then bust my ass looking for a political action replacement."

It sounded reasonable, and Norman started interviewing, but he couldn't find a replacement. That magnificent ego of his stood in his way. After all, who could do the job as well as Norman? He stayed on. My strategy worked. Instead of demonstrating my authority by denying his request—an authoritarian approach that I knew would alienate him—I set up a situation that would give me the desired results without dictating the outcome. I was creative in my approach, but having authority to fall back on gave me the security to be creative.

Authority can be lost not only through the strength of your adversaries, but also through the weak support of your allies. A negotiator who loses authority is left in an almost impossible situation. Never let it happen.

For the most part, the consumer holds the cards in everyday negotiations. The ability to choose from a number of retailers and service providers gives the consumer authority, at least theoretically. Of course, here, as elsewhere, your authority can be undercut. One of the ways is by an ally.

It is easy to overlook the potential pitfalls caused by an ally. You expect your adversary to work against you. You don't expect it from an ally. As difficult as it may be to be objective about an ally, particularly one who is close to you, you should not avoid preparation and strategizing because of that closeness. As the following example illustrates, you could find yourself totally subverted by that closeness. The issue in this case, the purchase of an item, is minor, but the circumstances are typical and can be an object lesson for all of us.

Betsy and I were in Oaxaca, Mexico, and Betsy saw two rugs she loved. The difference between the asking price and what I wanted to pay was very small, but not so small that I wanted to give in to the young seller. She saw immediately that Betsy really wanted those rugs, though, and the negotiations were over.

More in amusement than in logic, I kept the negotiations going.

This infuriated the seller, who justifiably felt the bargain was sealed. Señora wanted to pay the price. Señor certainly had no reason to haggle. Betsy was joining her in her impatience with me. I turned to Betsy and said, in English, "Betsy, let me enjoy myself."

Betsy was concerned that we could lose the rugs. I knew we wouldn't because, if necessary, I would give the woman her price. The difference was very small, and the negotiations weren't important. The same scenario can occur with higher stakes. In the purchase of a house, the chief negotiator can have a spouse who lets it be known that he or she wants a particular house no matter what. In such a situation, you become totally subverted. To avoid this, every couple should have a frank discussion about their differences prior to entering into negotiations. At a minimum, it will give you a positive feeling about the process. Most important, you can reduce or eliminate the surprises that may emerge as you negotiate.

In formal negotiations, a chief negotiator who feels everybody isn't on board will call a caucus. In negotiations involving family or friends, concerns should be put on the table prior to the negotiations. But one's position can change as nuances in terms of cost and the quality of the product or service emerge during the talks. There is nothing wrong with the chief negotiator's asking for time to discuss the matter in private with his or her spouse. This type of caucus is good for the negotiations and good for your relationships. And it can protect your innate authority as a consumer.

Subversion by an ally can be quite costly. I witnessed an example of this on a visit in 1984 to South Africa when I was doing some work for the Public Service International in Johannesburg. I was staying with Hank Slack, who was a chief negotiator with Anglo-American, the major conglomerate in South Africa. He told me about a disturbing breakdown in the negotiations between his firm and the National Mineworkers Union. The main players were two of the most talented young men in South Africa.

Bobby Godsell was the head of personnel and chief negotiator for Anglo-American. After a torturous strike, he came to an agreement with the mineworkers. Cyril Ramaphosa, who later became a political leader under Nelson Mandela, was head of the union.

Bobby defined the problem. Issues of amnesty, back pay, and re-hiring were already settled. The remaining problem was the mine directors. They were the most conservative faction of Anglo-American's management, and they refused to cooperate with the agreements that had been reached. They felt they were a power unto themselves and were asserting their authority. In doing so, they subverted Bobby's negotiating stance.

The labor-management relationship had deteriorated to a point where Cyril was not talking to Bobby. Bobby asked me if I would speak to Cyril. I called this very proud labor leader and asked him if he would meet with Bobby. "No way. Mr. Godsell betrayed me. There's no way I can trust him. It would be demeaning to go through another negotiation." I knew how angry Cyril was by his tone, and the fact that he was referring to Bobby as "Mr. Godsell."

I told Cyril that Bobby acknowledged the "betrayal" by management and that it had now been rectified. The mine directors took matters into their own hands and refused to carry out the amnesty agreement.

"Vic, I can't trust the management." In Cyril's view, Bobby's side had lost its authority and, with it, its credibility.

I then asked Cyril what he had to lose, and I explained the situation.

Cyril's members were suffering from the impasse; if the mine directors really wanted to betray him, they could launch a negative campaign against the union; Bobby's reaching out ensured that agreement could be consummated; a second betrayal would be too costly not only for Cyril, but for Bobby as well.

I spoke to Cyril as an old trade unionist who has had his share of betrayals. I explained that when strikes are over, relationships continue. Bobby's request for Cyril to resume the negotiations put Cyril in a position of strength. It increased his authority.

Finally, Cyril agreed to a private meeting and asked me to attend. These two young men, both in their thirties, did some of the best negotiating I have ever witnessed. Without signing any documents, they came to an iron-clad agreement. It was one of the rare moments in my career when I didn't say a word. As we were leaving, Cyril said, "Bobby, I appreciate this meeting." The negotiations ended on a first name basis. But they had nearly foundered over Bobby's loss of authority when one group in his organization refused to accept his leadership.

Using Authority

Betsy, with some anger, testifies against male society because of her insecurities at the beginning of her career. She says that her passiveness and acceptance of the mediocre diminished as her expertise and position grew. She says it loud and clear: "I would never have stood my ground years ago. If I withdraw now, it's on my own terms—not because of submissiveness."

A woman can also have authority, and magnificent authority, without a recognized professional career. There are some women whose authority rests in their satisfaction and love for children, husband, and household. The young housewife today insists that her husband participate around the house. (The younger generation of men are much more receptive to this than my generation. We copped out.) The change has come about in part because women at home use their authority. They insist the household needs male involvement and do not give their husbands the freedom to sit it out. This is a positive use of authority that women have developed.

Recognizing the importance of authority in negotiations is the first step in developing it. It can't be taught, but it can be understood and appreciated. At a minimum, by considering it as a factor before the negotiations begin, as well as during the talks, you will be better prepared to deal with whatever authority your adversary may bring to the table.

POWER

Tony Blair, the prime minister of England, defines power on a practical basis. In *The New York Times* of July 3, 1995, Blair stated, "Power without principle is barren, but principle without power is futile." I agree with this definition, provided it is carried out in practice.

In preparing for, and quite possibly again as the negotiations proceed, you need to assess your power position. Be as honest and objective as possible. If you overestimate your power, you will be in trouble; if you underestimate it, you will bring an unnecessary weakness upon yourself. Power need not be defined as aggressive strength. Sometimes the laid-back, accommodating person has a power that is not apparent.

A friend is an investment banker in a top firm specializing in the health services industry, specifically the business of buying and selling companies. He was involved in a major negotiation for the sale of a European company. The buyer was a multinational American organization.

On my friend's side of the table were the CEO of the European company, its attorney, and the major shareholder. My friend and the major shareholder shared the role of chief negotiator. Dual leadership is generally considered counterproductive, but it was not a concern to my friend.

The negotiators for the multinational group were its senior vice president, another vice president, and two attorneys.

The major issues were these:

- Protection of top personnel from layoffs
- The timing of the closing of the deal
- The method of payment
- The amount to be paid for the company

Both sides intelligently resolved the issues that were the most manageable, leaving the toughest for last. This creates a positive atmosphere and accelerates the negotiations toward a solution.

The personnel protection issue was no problem. The company agreed to keep the top people. After some intense negotiations, they also worked out the timing issue. My friend's reason for haste was that other potential buyers were in the background. He did not want to lose them, especially since other offers allowed him to bargain in strength. The other offers put him in the power position.

The method of payment became a key issue, and the negotiations became an all-day, all-night, all-morning affair. My friend remained strong and won out. This victory strengthened his position of power in negotiating the final and most important issue: the purchase price.

My friend's price was $350 million. The counteroffer was $200 million. My friend's bottom line was $300 million, so there was a long way to go. The negotiations were exhausting, but my friend got his price. He agreed to have the money paid in installments. His initial source of strength—having other buyers in the wings—when coupled with the method of payment victory allowed him to be aggressive without arrogance.

In other types of negotiations, the power position can be dictated by the socioeconomic environment. In buying or selling a house, the real estate market determines who is holding the cards. The real estate market, however, fluctuates relative to the overall economy and interest rates, as well as neighborhood conditions and even the season.

Betsy and I recently sold our brownstone in Brooklyn. Our roles had reversed, and with Betsy's career moving to the forefront, it was important that we move to Manhattan, closer to where she works. We put the house on the market in late spring, traditionally the best season to sell. The negotiations for a decent selling price were quite difficult. Out of nervousness, I was prepared to reduce the asking price.

Ralph Pepe, my real estate adviser, stepped into the situation and cautioned us to be patient. "After Labor Day the market will open up. There will be more interest in the house then." He was right.

The market began to open up, and so did the negotiations. Ralph's intelligence put Betsy and me in a more advantageous negotiating position. We received two very respectable offers. We were in a power position and could have used the competing offers to drive up the price of the house. I didn't want to take advantage of the situation and accepted an offer $50,000 higher than we had expected. The seasonal change in the housing market gave Betsy and me an excellent negotiating position. The power had shifted to us due to outside factors. (Once again, thanks, Ralph.)

If You Have It, Don't Flaunt It

If you have the power in negotiations, the best thing is not to talk about it. If you think you have a winner, don't advertise it to your adversary, much less to the world and media at large. This will only complicate and possibly even undermine the negotiations.

A few years ago, my friend Ed Silver and I were mediating an end to the Harvard Club strike in New York City. Ed was a senior partner from the prestigious law firm of Proskauer Rose. The Hotel and Restaurant Employees had struck over wages and workload. We had difficulty with a major leader of the union, who got angry and upset whenever management made an offer not to his liking. Our mediation came at the worst time—*after* a strike had already taken place. This is a difficult time for mediators to arrive on the scene and get involved. The adversaries had fixed positions, and there was little room for flexibility. When we arrived, the environment was one of anger and acrimony, and this young leader, boasting that he was going to win, and on his terms, was part of that environment. Ed took the young man in hand. He let him know there was nothing more counterproductive than this sort of boasting. Ed told him it was unnecessary language and reasoned that if he was going to win, the language wasn't needed, and if he didn't win, it would be embarrassing to him. Ed assured this young man it was much more important to look at the issues and contest those issues.

In a sense, the young man was bragging about his power, and the truth is, he did have it. The people he represented had been out on strike almost six months; they were unified and strong. This was the source of his power. Management was embarrassed by the strike; the publicity was not good, and they wanted the strike to end. But Ed was right; the young leader didn't have to flaunt his power. In most situations of this type when you are negotiating a conclusion to a strike, you have to weigh the hardship suffered by the workers against the hardship suffered by management. Management knew that the union leader had the support of these lower-income strikers. It was not necessary to hit them over the head with this fact. Eventually management agreed to settle on the union's terms. The union struck for additional manpower. More workers were added to the staff.

Getting angry can be helpful as a negotiating style, but in certain situations, anger is counterproductive, especially when you know you can make your point another way. The anger eventually has to give way to a strong discussion of the issues. If you do have the power, the sooner you get to those issues, the better. A powerful person doesn't necessarily have to be an aggressive one. A powerful person doesn't have to push principle and people out of his way. In fact, you can have power and be rather passive. Your position, rather than your personality, can make for power, as I mentioned earlier.

Mayor Rudy Giuliani negotiates very well when power is balanced. If he has the upper hand, he can be brutal. He will be more macho than Ed Koch and try to decimate his opposition. It may give him a persona of strength, but it can also backfire.

In dealing with the Legal Aid lawyers, the mayor pulled out all the stops. He forbade them the right to strike. He threatened to cut out their contractual raises. He demeaned the lawyers as a group in the press. He castigated them for using the strike weapon. In the mind of the mayor, "Lawyers should not strike."

The issue—the lawyers were deprived of a raise that top management had already received—did not call for this kind of behavior from the mayor. The situation was ripe for a solution. In fact, the lawyers folded, giving the new mayor a huge win. But a negotiation never stands alone. It is a continuing process. Giuliani made his mark as a macho negotiator, and his toughness set a managerial negotiating standard. His victory with the Legal Aid Society set up a bad situation in negotiations with the school bus drivers.

Giuliani took a public and determined stand against the seniority clause in the bus drivers' contract. He insisted that he was going to eliminate it since it inhibited the Board of Education's ability to obtain less expensive contracts. The Amalgamated Transit Union local let it be known this was a strike issue.

Giuliani prepared. He lined up replacements (scabs) to drive the students to schools if the strike occurred. But because of legal restrictions and other union resistance, not enough replacements were available in the event of a strike. The threat of a strike was power enough. The mayor then negotiated a settlement without eliminating the seniority clause. It was a fair settlement and a fair compromise. However, because of the mayor's previous macho stance and his strong language on the seniority issue, publicity made him seem a loser. He had backed down. In reality he was not a loser, but he appeared to be one because he had previously flaunted his power.

Giuliani's arrogance gained him grudging respect, although some of the public thought that he was overdoing it. As the November 1997 mayoral election approached, the mayor toned down a bit. He began to shed some of his rough edges, and his popularity and margin of support grew.

When You Don't Have Power

Chick Chaikin, a former president of the International Ladies Garment Workers Union, expressed his frustration at not being able to negotiate better fringe benefits and improved wages for his members because of their awkward economic position due to the impossible competition in international trade. The other union of clothing workers, the Amalgamated Clothing Workers of America, despite a proud history and leadership, also suffered at the bargaining table, weakened by the loss of power in a skewed competitive world.

International trade had decimated the ranks of the clothing workers as one factory after another shut down. Nevertheless, they had good organizers. I remember their organizer in Pennsylvania, a wonderfully dedicated human being who was depressed as all hell. He asked me, "How would you like to face the simple fact that almost every week there's a shutdown or a possible shutdown?" I assured him that it was an experience I would not relish. This situation did not provide for a good negotiating stance by the leadership of the Amalgamated Clothing Workers. Still, they looked for alternatives. They stayed at the bargaining table, and they explored politics and legislative lobbying. They were vilified as "protectionists" because they tried to protect the working conditions and livelihood of their members.

Unfortunately, this rearguard action could not offset the problems caused by the rise of the textile industries and clothing industries in the developing countries. U.S. factories had moved to such places as Pakistan, Indonesia, Malaysia, Thailand, India, and Central America, where wages ranged from twenty cents to one dollar an hour. When China entered the market, the wage structure worsened. A negotiating table cannot rectify the international trade imbalance.

The bargaining table for the needle trades unions had become an almost impossible and powerless place. This had little to do with labor leaders' abilities, which were excellent. It had little to do with the membership, which was unified and dedicated. It had mostly to do with the international trade system, which devastated important industries and made the union leadership almost powerless.

It is not always easy to accept the fact that in certain situations you are powerless. But there may be circumstances beyond your control that make negotiating impossible.

When You Have More Power Than You Realize

In a strike situation, the parties want a public forum where they can present a positive image and in the process make their adversaries look like the bad guys. Public support gives them power. In many cases, negative publicity encourages the defensive negotiators to close the talks so the public can't keep reading about how nasty they might be.

This is true of personal negotiations as well. A group of my friends were negotiating with a landlord, notorious for avoiding repairs and common services, who was neglecting their apartments. The negotiations dragged on for months, and he was immovable. They decided to go public, and they did it visually. They sent pictures to the press showing gaping holes in ceilings—excellent visual copy. One story accomplished what months of negotiating had failed to do. The landlord didn't want the publicity. He didn't become a model landlord, but he made the repairs, and the tenants began to live comfortably.

In a divorce where the participants are well known, bad publicity can put one or both parties on the defensive. Neither Ivana nor Donald Trump looked positive during their divorce. But since he was the more well known of the two, he took bigger public lumps. One major story in the papers about the problems of their children led to an end to the public war. The publicity was put on the back burner and the negotiations became private and more positive.

Here is another example of the power of the press. My friend Maurice suffered a terrible tragedy when his daughter and son-in-law were killed because the ferry they were on capsized in the English Channel. In his grief, looking for answers, Maurice researched the causes and soon discovered that British regulations governing ferry design were sorely lacking and had allowed a situation where an accident was just waiting to happen. The fact that the accident could have been avoided compounded Maurice's grief and impelled him on a mission to prevent a future tragedy.

The legally acceptable ferry standards were virtually worthless, allowing for open decks that could not sustain water penetration and minimal fire protection. The boat had capsized in ninety seconds, clearly an indication that proper safeguards were not met.

Maurice initially took his case to the owner of the ferry, but this was to no avail since the ferry met the meager specification standards. The responsible party was the Ministry of Transportation, the governmental body that produced and enforced the regulations, the body that had approved the ferry's faulty design. The Ministry would not talk to him. They had the power that comes with intractable bureaucracies and the "you can't fight City Hall" mind-set. But Maurice was determined. Hundreds of lives were lost in this incident. He continued his crusade by going to the media.

Maurice kept up an incessant barrage against the Ministry of Transportation. He mobilized others who had suffered losses in the sinking and documented their personal tragedies for the public. His newly formed committee lobbied politicians, presenting simple but compelling evidence of the wrongdoing. The lobbying began to pay off as the Ministry absorbed pressure from the legislature.

Pressure was also applied to the Institute of Naval Architects and the Royal Academy of Engineers. Maurice and his supporters reminded these organizations of their primary role and responsibility for public safety.

The Ministry of Transportation began to negotiate. It took three years for them to admit they had problems and seven additional years for the regulations to be changed. (Bureaucratic delay and procrastination are universal.)

In this case, the power of the press not only led to a successful outcome; it inspired the negotiations. In addition, another kind of power was in play here—the power of perseverance. Maurice had it, and it led to victory.

I recommend the public relations arena in very few instances. Some people find it difficult to go that route even if it gives them an advantage. A close friend who could have had a field day and gained a magnificent advantage in advance did not have the stomach to exploit the situation publicly. It does not mean that he was weak; he felt the gain too costly for him. This goes back to the point I make time and again: individual beliefs and needs give people different roads on which to travel.

My own strong belief is to keep negotiations out of the press and devoid of publicity. Once they become public, animosities are exacerbated, and they wound a continuing relationship. Again I emphasize my previous point: your adversary is somebody you must continue to live with. You may need each other in the future.

PRINCIPLE

Negotiations should not be defined only in terms of position and power. Your belief in the correctness of your arguments gives you strength. I remember my complaint to Lillian Roberts, my executive assistant, in regard to a grievance concerning adequate dressing facilities: "Lil, why are you making such a fuss over this?"

Lillian faced me and responded, "Because it's the right thing to do." She went on to explain that our people deserved comfort and convenience as much as management did. Then she ended: "We're right, and we shouldn't back off." I learned from Lillian. Principle is not only part of the negotiations, it *is* the negotiations.

INTELLECTUAL ABILITY

A negotiator can never be too knowledgeable. Your own intelligence is terribly important, but if you don't have it, you hire it or you acquire it. You can't really be without it. Equally important is knowing your adversary's level of intelligence. In this regard the late Chicago mayor Richard J. Daley had an asset that put him in a formidable position: people underestimated his intelligence, and he could defeat his adversaries because of their underestimation of him.

Intelligence and authority often go hand in hand. Intelligence gives you authority, especially when it includes a working knowledge of your adversary's negotiating style.

One of Betsy's and my closest friends is a brilliant woman who lives in a man's world. Because of sexism, she typically has to assess and conform her negotiating position to the circumstances. At one of her client companies, she has to negotiate completely with two senior executives, and her approach with each of them varies demonstrably.

She knows that the CEO disdains negotiations; with him, her requests are either approved on the spot, or she is told to go back to the drawing board. Since she is paid on a project-by-project basis, she carefully considers each fee before approaching the CEO. She buttresses her requests with information about the time required for each project, the importance of the project, and the value of the project to the firm. He usually accepts her numbers without any question. She has established a negotiating stance with him that is justified by her work and ability.

The number-two man in the firm never accepts her first offer, so she does traditional negotiating with him. She keeps her bottom line in her mind and carefully thinks out the steps to reach it. Her first figure therefore is based on the need to reach her bottom line ultimately. The negotiations are always drawn out, but she never fails to reach her bottom line.

She has an excellent mind and an excellent understanding of her adversaries. Her negotiations just about always have positive outcomes.

Know When to Reach Out

Sometimes your intelligence doesn't match the challenge, and you may need professional assistance. Too many of us are reluctant to reach out—a foolish and sometimes tragic mistake.

A close friend was a workaholic. Totally immersed in his job, he neglected his family. After five years, they had had a couple of children, and his wife understandably expected his participation in the household and in their life as a family. They argued over this, and the marriage began to rock.

It had no impact on him. His work was his life, and he saw no need to negotiate or compromise. Betsy recommended family therapy, but this recommendation was not enough to move him. He was immune to the negative effects of his behavior. The axe fell. In no uncertain terms, his wife told him she was going to leave.

In shock and surprise, he turned to Betsy, who confirmed his wife's intentions. He now accepted the fact that he needed outside help. Through therapy, he began to listen, communicate, and negotiate. He is still a workaholic, but now he makes certain there is time for his family.

Another friend was quite ill with cancer. His wife was totally distressed because he did not seem to face the fact that he had the disease and did not seek treatment. Since her husband was not responding to her pleas, she asked a friend who was close to both of them for help. The friend met with him. He did not mince words: "Eddie, you're a selfish son of a bitch. All you give a damn about is yourself. I don't mind if you go down the drain, but look at what you're doing to those who love you. You are responsible for others, and you don't give a shit."

The friend used shock negotiations. Eddie knew he had a tiger by the tail who would not let up. My friend's toughness was combined with intelligence—an unbeatable combination. There are negotiations where you have to vulgarize the other person's self-interest. It does work.

KNOWING YOUR LIMITATIONS

In order to grow and develop into a good negotiator, you must recognize that nobody has it all. You should be aware of your limitations—not accepting of them, but aware of them so you can diminish their effect. (My own shortcomings include reacting too emotionally, which sometimes negates my intelligence.) By admitting to mistakes, you can cut your losses sooner and more effectively. This is not easy, particularly for labor leaders, because our egos get in the way. But it is far better to be able to admit a mistake and correct it.

Even Mayor Koch, who has a big ego and would brag about the fact that "my mother didn't raise dumb sons," would admit to mistakes—but not often. He could change his top appointees when necessary and take a closer look at his administration. This is not the case with Rudy Giuliani. He finds it almost impossible to admit a mistake. His inability to take himself lightly at appropriate times has become legend. The mayor has had huge public rows with former schools chancellor Ramon Cortines and with former police commissioner William J. Bratton, which damaged his public standing because he would not acknowledge his limitations, among them his huge ego and use of bullying tactics.

Now, in the second term of Giuliani's administration, we in New York City are still waiting for him to admit to any major error. This is unfortunate because this kind of attitude can make you look as though you suffered a defeat when in reality you didn't.

In everyday negotiations, parents may not recognize their children's limitations and, with all good intentions, can set them on the road to failure. But unrealistic expectations cannot be met through negotiations. A child who is falling behind in school may need more than a family meeting where he is told to spend less time watching television and more time doing homework and studying. The child may have learning disabilities, emotional problems, or involvement with drugs. It may be difficult for the parents to accept this. But unless parents recognize their children's limitations, they may fail to find the real solutions to their problems.

It is important to know your limitations. And it is equally important, in view of those limitations, to cut any losses that might ensue. As a negotiator, you are not always expected to win. There will be times when you have salutary negotiations based on cutting your losses. Sometimes you are in a difficult situation, and the most you can do is to rectify some of that situation. There is nothing wrong with this.

SENSITIVITY

Like intelligence, your level of sensitivity—your understanding of and appreciation for the attitudes and feelings of others—is a major part of who you are, you cannot leave it at the door of the negotiating room. Your degree of empathy coupled with your specific personal prejudices will surely have an impact on the outcome of the negotiations. You should make every effort to recognize your strengths and weaknesses in this area.

I had to negotiate a grievance in the Chicago Board of Education. An African American member of the union had filed charges against a white supervisor who demeaned her. The contrast between the black grievant and the white supervisor was compelling.

Our black member was well dressed and soft spoken. The supervisor was a loud, offensive slob. Nevertheless, the supervisor complained of the unkempt dress and the behavior of our member. No specifics were put on the table. The personnel director who handled the situation for the Board of Education was visibly embarrassed. He tried in vain to obtain some rationale from the supervisor.

The supervisor's racism was painfully apparent and blocked any positive negotiating. We won the case, but in the Chicago of 1957, the supervisor was not admonished. If the loss to management was considered at all, it was considered an isolated incident.

Here is an example of a tough negotiation a friend participated in where sensitivity saved the day when reason and compromise could not.

The employees had already demonstrated to their supervisor that through some creative scheduling, one person per department could use vacation days to extend the Christmas or New Year's holiday on the condition that the person commit to working one holiday or the other. Until this time, employees were not allowed to take vacation time at all between December 15 and January 15 since this was the company's busiest season.

At a meeting of employees and the three supervisors, one of the supervisors went to the chalkboard and started to draw a mock schedule. Her contention was that no department would be able to fill in the scheduling gaps if one employee was on vacation. Since she was the supervisor in charge of scheduling, the other administrators relied on her expertise while debating this proposal. But no matter what she tried, she couldn't demonstrate that scheduling changes couldn't address the request of the workers. It became obvious that by scheduling in part-timers, it *was* possible for one employee to take vacation time without compromising a department.

The head supervisor, her face red with embarrassment but her mouth set in grim determination, turned to the group and said, "It just isn't done. Employees of this company have never been allowed to take vacation at Christmas or New Year's." She was known throughout the company as a stubborn, closed-minded woman.

Suddenly one of the employees spoke up: "May I say something? A few years ago, my mother was very ill, and my family decided to have one more Christmas together in Barbados. It had been years since my mother had us all home for Christmas, and it would probably be the last time. My request for vacation was denied. I didn't go. I couldn't afford to lose my job. I was newly widowed with a son in college. My mother died that year. I beg you to consider this proposal."

There was silence around the table. Then one of the supervisors, tears in her eyes, spoke: "We would like to caucus for a few minutes." She nodded to the other supervisors, and they got up and left the room.

A few minutes later the three weary supervisors filed back into the room.

"Proposal accepted. Thank you for reminding us that it is not only the clients that matter. The employees matter too."

My friend recalls this as one of the most important things she has ever been part of. It was exhilarating and joyful, and as successful as negotiations can get.

Chapter Two

ASSESSING YOUR ADVERSARY

Every negotiation is a confrontation—a conflict, a clashing of forces or ideas . . . a challenge. As you begin each negotiation, you will need to develop a feel for your adversary and the negotiating style he or she brings to the table. The primary indicator of style will be how each of the players deal with, or does not deal with, confrontation at the bargaining table.

Understanding your own and your adversary's attitude toward confrontation will give you the clearest signal of the style and character of the negotiations to come. My own feeling is that confrontation is essential to negotiations and should not be avoided. It is, however, a double-edged sword that requires skillful handling. If you have too much confrontation, negotiations will suffer. Excessive confrontation signals that something is wrong with the negotiators, the process, the principles, and the road to solution. But if you exclude confrontation, you will have no therapy, no real progress or solutions, because the issues will not get on the table. The result of this situation is what I refer to as nonnegotiating.

Nonconfrontationalists fall into two basic types: the passive and the authoritarian. They avoid confrontation for different reasons, but both types undermine the negotiating process itself. For me, lack of confrontation is even more counterproductive than a negotiation that has been reduced to a shouting match.

Your willingness to be confrontational and ability in this area will determine how effectively you employ this critical tool. Specific circumstances and interpersonal relationships will also affect your style. You use different styles with different people or conditions. Your adversary's negotiating persona may be quite different from his or her general demeanor. It may also vary from negotiation to negotiation.

People often view themselves, or are viewed by others, as being either confrontational or nonconfrontational. You must go beyond this simple definition in order to become a better negotiator. You need to examine the specific situation, your adversary's style, and your own comfort level with confrontation. Experience and practice will make you more comfortable with negotiating. But the first step is developing a willingness to confront the issues. Without this willingness by at least one of the parties, there are no negotiations. This is particularly true in personal negotiations.

Your Willingness to Confront

Close friends had an excellent marriage. He was a successful entrepreneur. She was content with her role as traditional housewife. They had three children, and he was a devoted father, always spending quality time with the family despite the distractions of a successful and growing business. Because they could afford the help she needed with the household, she had the freedom to involve herself in numerous cultural activities—theater, opera, sculpture. Her greatest pleasure was her family life, and she always felt secure about being an important part of her husband's life. He discussed both personal and business problems with her, and he valued her advice. There were arguments and disagreements, of course, but they relished their ability to communicate with each other. Suddenly, he was silent, and the communication stopped.

Thrown by his withdrawal, she tried talking to him, but there was no response, and she found herself surrendering to the withdrawal symptoms. They did their best to keep the kids out of the gloom. Periodically, she would make an attempt to communicate to find out what the problem was, but to no avail.

I told her that she had to do something very uncharacteristic to get him to open up: she had to confront him because something was going on that was depressing the hell out of him.

"Vic, I can't do it. I adore him, and I'm afraid it will upset him more."

I told her she was too unhappy to allow the situation to continue. If he was not letting her in, her whole life was turned around. She admitted the situation was worsening, and she was becoming more depressed with each day of silence. The simple fact was that she had to bring him to the negotiating table and not let go.

"You don't have to be angry," I told her, "and you should avoid being too emotional, but you must make clear that you want an explanation of his behavior over the past months. You should not let him off the hook without an answer."

She mulled over my advice, then moved in on him after a few more weeks of deadly silence. Having finally made up her mind, she was exceptionally resolute. He tried to rationalize by telling her the situation wasn't really as bad as she was describing it.

In calm but definitive language, she assured him the situation *was* bad. She felt shut out and would not accept a peripheral response. She needed to hear what was wrong. He was evasive, got angry, and was ready to stalk out of the room.

She didn't budge and zinged him: "Daniel, if you leave, we won't talk about anything. I've had it. There will be no further attempt to communicate with you."

Her reaction was so atypical for her that he froze in his tracks. He looked straight into her eyes. She didn't budge. He sat down and began to open up.

It turned out that this incredibly successful man was on the economic defensive for the first time. His business was suffering dramatic losses, and he couldn't get a handle on it. She asked him specific questions about his junior partners and their relationship given the downturn in the business. He described it in full detail. He felt they were loyal but understandably critical of him. He spoke about the reasons for the decline in the business and some of the clients he had lost.

The conversation was terribly difficult for him at first, but it became easier as they went along. She knew a great deal about his work and realized he was in big trouble. Then a strange paradox occurred: the more agitated he became, the more relaxed she was. After hours of discussion and give-and-take, she embraced him and said, "Daniel, there are times when I want to be wanted. You've been a magnificent father and husband. I'm not here just to reap the rewards. It's all very simple: I adore you."

He responded in kind.

As it turned out, his business recovered. More important, he recovered, as did their marriage. One can only imagine what the outcome would have been had she not been willing to confront him head on.

An objective opinion from a trusted ally can often change a situation dramatically. The advice you receive may be a few simple sentences long, as it was with a friend who was overwhelmed by an extremely negative relationship with her boss. She did not see confrontation as an option or strategy in resolving the situation. I assured her it was.

She had been recently widowed and was in a fragile emotional state. At work, she had reached the breaking point and called me to say that she had made up her mind to resign. I knew how much she loved the work she was doing, and how much she needed satisfaction on the job. With the sudden and recent death of her husband, she was lonely and insecure. She didn't need the aggravation at work caused by her boss's inexplicable and unjustifiable attacks. She had tried openly and calmly to discuss his dissatisfaction with her, but he refused to meet with her. He continued to undermine her authority with her staff, making it impossible for her to perform her job. He had cut her out of the information loop and assigned subordinates to represent him at meetings she held.

I agreed that she could not perform her job without his support, but my response to her was simply, "Don't quit. Now that you've decided to quit, you have nothing to lose by standing up to him." She responded, "I don't have the strength to fight. I'm a basket case emotionally." I said, "Then don't fight. On those days when you can't bear to face him, don't go to work. Do whatever you have to do, but don't quit. He can't fire you. If he could, he would have already done so." This woman had an impeccable reputation in her field. I knew it, and I knew that he knew it. He had, after all, recruited her for the job.

From that moment on, my friend's attitude changed. Her own decision to quit, coupled with my advice, gave her the strength she needed to fight. She was now willing to be confrontational.

She began to respond in writing to his nasty memos and asked subordinates to leave meetings they had no reason for attending except to unnerve her. On the rare occasions when her boss held staff meetings that included her, she made a conscious effort to speak with authority and confidence. She openly challenged her boss's arbitrary and superficial criticisms of her ideas and reports.

This story has a happy ending. As soon as she changed her attitude, she stopped feeling victimized and no longer dreaded going to work. Her boss's attacks diminished. A few months later, her boss was fired; the new CEO did not believe he had adequate leadership skills. Neither one of us was surprised.

My friend often credits me with preventing her from making a terrible mistake. I remind her that she was the one who reached out for help. Getting outside help was the beginning of the solution in her case. She sought what she needed as she assessed her adversary. This is an important step for novice negotiators in general.

Healthy Confrontation

My relationship with Ed Koch is a perfect example of how confrontation can be healthy and positive. I could be presumptuous and say that I got what I wanted, but the truth is even more rewarding than that. Although the negotiations were fierce, I always felt that the people I represented were pleased with the outcomes, and Koch, his staff, and the public were pleased too.

To a large extent, my knowledge and understanding of his style led to the positive results. I knew that in certain situations, I should avoid dealing directly with him, and since the mayor had excellent people around him, I would look for other members of the staff with whom to negotiate. You have this luxury when you represent the largest union in the city and you also have this luxury when you're dealing with the mayor who represents that city. There are other outlets, other people, other ways of getting to the issues.

I used this approach during my first grievance negotiations with Ed Koch. He wanted to wipe out a group of street workers, who happened to be mainly Hispanic. The union didn't quarrel with his decision; our argument was simply that the workers could be retrained and ought not to be put out on the unemployment line. Koch became belligerent and called our proposal ridiculous. It was too costly, and he couldn't accept it. I was prepared for this response.

My colleague Lillian Roberts had already worked out a training program using grants and state money that would provide these workers with training for different jobs. Koch, however, responded with what I regarded as a silly point: "Well, the taxpayers still have to pay for it whether it's state money or not." Previous mayors usually agreed with us that the state exploited the city and that anything that we could get back from the state would be fair. I tried to make this point, but Koch wouldn't listen.

He then turned on me and said, "Don't tell *me* that I can't fire people!" In exasperation I replied, "This really has nothing to do with firing people. What it has to do with is the needs of these people and the needs of the city, and I think we can homogenize it. Put it together. Nobody questions your right, Ed, to lay off these workers." But he became more belligerent, used some unkind words, and cut off any more discussion.

So I went to Herman Badillo, one of the deputy mayors. (Koch's ego never prevented him from appointing talented staffers.) Herman and I worked it out, or at least agreed to the parameters. Then Lillian Roberts and others fit the pieces together. We had saved the jobs of some 180 street workers.

This, in a sense, was typical of my relationship with Koch: stubborn, almost vulgar toward each other, but we were both willing to confront the issues. We understood each other. In negotiating with Koch, I brought the issues to the table through direct confrontation, but the agreements were reached indirectly, with the help of our staffs. In the years that I negotiated against him and his administration, we somehow came up with solutions. Koch would call me the "pits" and I would call him a "pseudo-macho bastard." We never said the words to each other directly, but he made sure they got back to me, and I made sure they got back to him.

For negotiations involving family members or friends, the issues can be clouded or complicated by the relationship. An objective party may be needed not only to identify the issues but to confront them. This was the case with a restaurateur who was negotiating with his cousin—and potential landlord.

Marty's cousin owned a building with two restaurants, one of them vacant. Marty had previously run restaurants, and his cousin offered him the space. He now needed a chef and found Lucy, who was as tough as she was lovely. They began negotiating with his cousin.

The cousin wanted a major piece of the profits. In addition, he insisted on some restrictions regarding the number of tables, his arbitrary right to relocate their business, and his approval of staff. Because of the family relationship, Marty's response was subdued. Lucy watched the proceedings. In private, she told Marty that his cousin was exploiting him. She suggested they take a different approach. "Let's just follow normal procedures. We'll renovate the space and pay him rent."

At first Marty held back. This was his cousin, and he didn't want to be confrontational. But Lucy was persistent. She told Marty that his cousin was loading the dice in his favor. Besides, her suggestion was standard and fair and consistent with other business deals of this nature.

Intuitively, Lucy knew that Marty had to separate his personal feelings from the business negotiations. She felt that the cousin was a materialistic operator who did not share Marty's sense of family loyalty. Marty began to see the light.

When they presented their counterproposal to the cousin, they discovered the cousin was not the sole owner of the building. The cousin had a partner with a controlling interest—*and* veto power over everything. They now decided to negotiate with Artie, the real power, the controlling interest. The cousin was out.

They agreed with Artie to start off small. It would be a take-out restaurant. They also agreed on the rent, the length of the lease, and a guarantee against a similar restaurant's opening in the building. When Artie and his lawyers put their agreement in writing, the safeguards were not in it, so the diminutive and sweet Lucy took over, confronting both Artie and the attorneys.

Marty was incredibly impressed with Lucy. Respect turned to love. A double deal was consummated: they opened the restaurant and got married. Healthy confrontation at its best!

Unhealthy Confrontation

There is only one thing worse than nonconfrontation, and that is confrontation for the sake of confrontation, or bullying. This usually happens when relationships are breaking down—where the desire for revenge becomes the motivation, as in a bad marriage.

At dinner, I was seated next to a friend whose marriage was on the rocks. It was public knowledge that the marriage was on the way down, and as is typically the case, the friends get to know the anger but not the real reasons for the breakup.

He rejected her. He was a known womanizer and had disparaged her publicly. She was terribly angry and responded in kind. They both upped the negative ante. She didn't have a decent thing to say about him. The negotiator in me asked her, "Have you ever tried to talk it out?" She replied, "It's useless. We always find ourselves using invective and getting at each other."

To my next question, "Have you tried to get outside help?" her reply was no more positive: "We've gone through counselors and therapists. It's a dead end. Nobody helps." My final question was this: "Why the hell do you keep going? Your kids are grown; you can live comfortably apart. It makes no sense."

It turned out that both had a need to continue the confrontation, and the bitterness continued for years. The senseless confrontation had become part of their lives.

Like bad marriages, souring business partnerships are commonplace. The unnecessary confrontation blocks any possibility of decent negotiations that could make healthy, profitable partnerships. Business partnerships, like marriages, are most successful when there is a mutual respect for each other's abilities. Even with this mutual respect, the road can be rocky, but the ability to discuss, to negotiate, to get an understanding of the other person's position, is key to positive relationships and outcomes—the goal of all negotiations.

THE NONCONFRONTATIONAL

Passive-Aggressives

In the New York City fiscal crisis of 1975, a moratorium on debt that would have saved the city $820 million was declared illegal by the courts, which forced the city to negotiate with the bankers to resolve the situation. I hadn't dealt with commercial bankers before, and as the chief negotiator for the unions I was hoping to have some input and to get additional funding from them. I focused my strategy for the negotiations around the issues and was prepared to confront my adversaries with the facts. I was expecting to be challenged, and I was expecting a heated debate. I knew little about the bankers themselves; they were an unknown quantity to me at the time. I was soon to learn a valuable lesson that augmented my knowledge in preparing for negotiations.

On one side of the table were the commercial bankers. They were Alfred Brittain III of Bankers Trust. There was Walter Wriston, the head of Citibank, the most powerful commercial banker at that time. There were Pat Patterson, the head of Morgan Guaranty, and David Rockefeller, the head of Chase Manhattan. These were terribly civilized men. On the other side of the table were McFeeley, Bigel, Gotbaum, Vizzini, Feinstein, a fairly outspoken group of labor leaders who minced no words, however vulgar. You had the WASP bankers on one side, the ethnics on the other.

At first, the negotiations moved in a proper direction. We put some issues on the table and Wriston, the chief spokesman, said, "Well, that sounds reasonable." We would then move on to the next issue, and he would say again, "This seems reasonable to me," and we would move on. After hours of negotiations, I felt optimistic. The adversaries seemed cooperative, even helpful. Hell, this looked great.

After these meetings, we met in the Blue Room of City Hall to summarize our position. I arrived at the Blue Room. Mayor Abe Beame was there, and I could see that he was troubled. Abe is very short, and he had almost shrunk into himself. He said, "Victor, read this." It was a summary from the bankers. They had not moved an inch. We were at the same place we started. The negotiations had been meaningless, and I was physically and emotionally exhausted. The fiscal crisis was not an easy time for anybody. It meant thousands of job losses to our members and incredible sacrifice on the union's part. We had to save a city from falling into default and literally becoming a municipal supplicant. I responded emotionally to a financial tragedy all New Yorkers faced: loss of jobs, prestige, and power. At that moment, I did not have the right to be overwhelmed, but I was overwhelmed. I took the bankers' paper, looked at it, and threw it at Wriston, telling him, "Shove it up your ass."

I was absolutely furious and walked out. Jack Bigel followed me, and we took turns calming each other. He suggested I return to the room because we just couldn't break it off. I used more vile language and told him I would not go back. I had to get the hell out. He agreed but reminded me that we would have to deal with them whether I liked it or not. Even though I didn't like it, Jack made sense. I tried to relax for the rest of the day and went home thinking that at least I would get some comfort from Betsy. What a mistake!

When I told Betsy what happened, she looked at me and said, "How could you be so stupid!" (I really didn't need this.) "Victor, these are my people. They were not playing games with you or leading you astray. That is the way they are: polite. They don't like confrontation. They were not going to disagree with you. What they were doing is what they do best. They act courteous and civilized, all the while doing as they please."

Betsy was right, of course, but I didn't understand it. I had failed to follow some cardinal rules of negotiations. You have to know your adversary, which I didn't, and you cannot act on emotion. I was not accustomed to this behavior.

We were never going to get real new money from the bankers, so what I had to do was to cut my losses and figure out where to go. What would the unions do? What would the city do? The bankers were not going to move because they did not have to; they held the cards and the most advantageous position in the negotiations. They didn't have to move, and they didn't. They wanted to avoid default, but it was not important enough for them to risk more money to do it. Default could mean the loss of fifty thousand to seventy-five thousand union jobs. It could jeopardize pension funds. The loss to our membership could be catastrophic. Our stakes were much too high to allow default to take place for the multitude of workers and their families.

In the chapter on preparing for major negotiations (Chapter 5), I give a detailed account of the union's contribution in resolving the fiscal crisis. It was monumental—far and away a greater sacrifice than that of the bankers or of any other group, including the federal and state governments.

In some cases, your adversary's passive (as opposed to passive-aggressive) nonconfrontational style can be quite beneficial to you. Herb Haber, Mayor John Lindsay's chief negotiator, played it straight and was very protective of Lindsay's interests. He protected those interests but resisted fighting for them. He saw his role more as a mediator than negotiator. Herb really didn't like to negotiate. His approach would be one in which "we are all in this together and we have to find a solution."

In one sense he was fortunate since I needed a Lindsay administration that was friendly. Lindsay and I were both new kids on the block at the time, and it was to our mutual benefit to get along. He knew it, and I knew it. So Herb was an excellent choice as chief negotiator for the mayor. In his case lack of confrontation was helpful—helpful for the city and helpful for the workers we represented. Neither of us wanted to make the other look bad. I had many enemies when I first came to New York, and I didn't need a confrontation with the mayor. John Lindsay, a most unusual mayor, was not only a Republican. He was an Anglo-Saxon Protestant with an aristocratic character in an ethnically and racially diverse and mostly Democratic city. And he was far too handsome. He was a perfect target for everybody to take aim at. So when it came to confrontation, neither of us needed or wanted it.

Authoritarians

The authoritarians are nonconfrontationists whose behavior presents a curious contradiction. Their methods of confrontation preclude discussion, disagreement, or any other form of response. They differ from passive people who avoid all confrontation. Some of the most successful nonconfrontationists are vulgar authoritarians who can, if it suits them, be charming as all hell.

The authoritarians use all means to stultify negotiations. They can be dishonest; they can use brutal aggression; they cow the opposition by establishing an environment of fear. Under rare circumstances, they withdraw rather than negotiate. Underneath, they are terribly insecure. Losing is something they fear.

On the other hand, if you go along, they are generous and dispense largesse. The payoff is material. One must give to them total, loyal devotion, and they will give you back anything but dignity.

Richard J. Daley was considered the last of the big city bosses for good reason. His powers and control were complete; he was a man in charge. An opposing Republican party was almost nonexistent. He had the support of State Street—the financial area—and the labor movement. He dispensed largesse. He was a man who believed in rewarding friends and punishing enemies, and he operated with Machiavellian brilliance. He rewarded his labor supporters with patronage and an increasing membership. The unions did not have to organize. Daley just turned over large numbers of city employees to friendly unions. The unions received automatic membership; the mayor received automatic political endorsement and support. Much to my regret, I discovered this at a Chicago labor meeting.

The meeting openly debated endorsing Daley. What was unbelievable is that the Republicans had not chosen their candidate. There were nine speakers in favor of the mayor and one person against him. I was that person. I appealed to the trade union principles of the group by saying that our union had no right to collective bargaining and no grievance procedure. Dues were collected by hand, a counterproductive way of stabilizing the finances of the union. I explained that although Daley was mayor and had done well for them, he was terrible for the people I represented. They listened impassively, then voted. I lost by 400 to 1.

When the meeting adjourned and I left the room, many of the old industrial unionists who agreed with me spoke in soft voices about how pleased they were that I had introduced my point. They were pleased, yet I couldn't get their vote. Daley's power was overwhelming.

Daley did not negotiate. He dispensed largesse. He gave his friends anything they wanted but a voice in his administration. He ruled almost without opposition because opposing him was meaningless. There were wonderful people who held on to dignity, such as Leon Despres, a councilman who would not play the game. He opposed Daley and made some of the best speeches I had ever heard on the floor of the City Council. What was good about Despres's opposition was that it irritated the hell out of Richard Daley, despite the fact that Despres could not win a vote. I learned from Leon.

Since I could not give the workers bread through negotiations, I gave them circuses. We had some of the most colorful protest rallies, and at every opportunity, the union would publicly criticize the mayor. My frustration was that the rallies brought little material gain from the mayor. His frustration was his own inability to tolerate any criticism. Even though we could make no inroads into his power, we had the satisfaction of knowing that we could unnerve him. This temporary satisfaction was all that I ever received from the mayor of Chicago.

Daley's unwillingness to negotiate or deal with opposition might have cost Hubert Humphrey the presidency. At the 1968 Democratic Convention, Daley's police brutalized the press and the student protestors. When Senator Abraham Ribicoff and others appealed to him to civilize the situation, he refused. He would curse, make anti-Semitic remarks, allow for a chaotic situation. He would do everything but negotiate. Vice President Humphrey lost the presidency by a small margin. Daley's refusal to negotiate at the convention created terrible publicity that might have given Nixon the presidency.

There are more subtle nonconfrontational authoritarians than Mayor Daley, as this example shows. Nonprofit organizations often seek private consultants to assist them in developing their long-term strategic plans, capital plans, and marketing strategies. Typically, nonprofit organizations are viewed as "doing the good work," and they expect that their altruistic posture entitles them to receive services at a reduced fee. This altruism can lead to arrogance and authoritarianism in negotiations.

In a negotiation with a nonprofit, a friend, a partner in a consulting firm specializing in planning for nonprofits, found himself in a lose-lose situation. His firm had a policy of charging nonprofits reduced rates, and he believed that was one of the reasons he had been asked to submit a proposal to this social service agency. The agency was interested in developing a marketing strategy to address the emergence of managed care companies, the potential competition. They told my friend they were prepared to spend $40,000 for the study. He submitted a $38,000 proposal to the agency's marketing committee and the chairman of the agency.

The negotiations with the marketing committee seemed to be going well. Subsequently, my friend received a call from the organization's executive director, who offered my friend $25,000 for phases one and two of the proposal. The offer was reasonable, and my friend agreed. Then the executive director added that the chairman of the organization insisted that the first two phases include three times as many interviews and other data collection. Claiming to be a good guy himself, the executive director told my friend there was a faction of the agency's board who questioned the project. My friend then realized he was not negotiating with the decision-makers and requested a negotiating meeting with the powers that be. He hoped to be able to explain how unreasonable it was to expect additional work without additional compensation.

The executive director and most of the marketing committee embraced his plan and were ready to raise his fee. The chairman would hear nothing of it. He wanted the additional work for free, and that was that.

My friend held another meeting, this one buttressed with materials supporting the need for the project. He told them they were jeopardizing for the agency a lucrative future market for a nominal sum—in short, penny wise and pound foolish. But the chairman played it hard and refused to budge, even after my friend went back to the drawing board and presented a bare-bones plan and compensation package. The chairman made no counteroffer or counterargument, for that matter. He simply used his authority and called the shots, while the executive director and marketing committee were silent and powerless participants.

My friend knew the project could not be successfully completed for $25,000 and turned it down. He was an ethical man and hoped the refusal would bring them back to the table. I advised him that this was unlikely so long as the chairman remained. I also told him that he had missed an opportunity in the negotiations that may have made a difference in the outcome.

In his early discussions with the executive director and the marketing committee, he had failed to identify the real power and the personality of that power. Those who were in favor of proceeding with the project could have been helpful in steering my friend through the process. His initial proposal could have been crafted differently, specifically addressing the chairman's desire for additional data collection up front. For the most part, nonconfrontational authoritarians tend to view compromise as losing. They are not likely to change course. At best, you get one shot with them.

The real sadness in the case of the authoritarians, be it the mayor of Chicago or the chairman of a nonprofit organization, is that there can be no future with them. You are either in a state of war or you must become terribly submissive. You cannot have a constructive, progressive role in anything they control unless you accept what they put on the table.

More About the Nonconfrontational Authoritarian

There is a double chorus from the play *Flower Drum Song*. The younger generation and older generation of Chinese families bemoan the fact they really don't talk the same language. They converse without communication. When this occurs in negotiations, it can be fatal.

The disastrous baseball negotiations of 1994 are an excellent example of noncommunicating. The owners insisted on a salary cap. Negotiations ensued, but it was soon apparent that management would not move. It was a prime example of noncommunication.

Coming to the table with an ultimatum, can lead to a disastrous conclusion. I'm always concerned when somebody on the other side of the table insists they must have this, or else. Even if an organization is on the verge of bankruptcy and it makes a demand it considers unalterable, that is a cardinal mistake. It is far better to work with an adversary to try to prevent a shutdown.

Noncommunication is senseless. It negates the meaning of negotiations. Nobody benefits when either side allows a breakdown.

Years of negotiating have convinced me that a solution is always possible. Within a given negotiation, both sides should avoid "this is my final offer; take it or leave it." It smacks too much of unconditional surrender.

There is a method of nonnegotiating called Boulwarism, named after a past CEO of General Electric, who refused to negotiate with the unions. His first offer was his final offer. Admittedly, the package he put on the table was at times very attractive. But for the union to accept management's first offer weakened and alienated the union. The union appeared to have no voice in the settlement, regardless of how positive it was. Management unilaterally decided the outcome of the negotiations.

There are many others who practice Boulwarism. My friend Oscar de la Renta told me of a negotiation with another designer that concerned Oscar's service over a given period of time. They had worked out expenses and benefits; then the main issue, compensation, came front and center.

Oscar gave him a round figure. The other designer defined this as a bargaining point and made a counteroffer. Oscar, who mixes sophistication and toughness with gentility, assured the gentleman this was exactly his price. It unnerved the other designer. If Oscar had asked for more and come down, life would have been so much easier for the other negotiator. He unhappily accepted Oscar's only offer.

Larry Tisch had a different situation. He also practices Boulwarism. In his ventures, he has in his mind a single and final price. This is not to be confused with having a bottom line. With a bottom line, you negotiate as close to your figure as possible. Larry Tisch believes that his price is fair and that he is not taking advantage of the person on the other side of the table. While he can be a tough, dogmatic person, Larry is also one of the straightest people I know. He does not talk for effect and is conservative in his beliefs. This man who built a multibillion-dollar conglomerate is strangely paradoxical; in negotiating he is basically a nonconfrontationist.

He wanted to sell the publishing arm of CBS. Jovanovich of Harcourt Brace Jovanovich was interested in buying. They met, and Jovanovich put his offer on the table: $500 million, in cash. In a matter of seconds, Larry Tisch put out his hand and said they had a deal.

When I asked Larry what he would have done if Jovanovich had offered him less than $500 million, he said, "I would have told him that was my price." He went on to assure me that he believed in a fair price and he loved to deal with people who played it straight. It served him well.

Boulwarism has its place in personal relationships. A friend of mine was in an ongoing courtship—or I should say, a prolonged courtship. They had been going together for years and had a positive and lovely relationship. They had discussed just about every detail of their future marriage, but the man had an agile mind matched by an agile tongue and was a genius at avoiding the topic of when the event would take place. He was estranged from his wife. They had had a difficult and unhappy marriage and he was reluctant to tie the knot again. He loved her—but . . .

My friend was quite traditional and found the state of unmarriage, and lack of movement toward it, most unnerving. Her demands grew in direct proportion to her frustration. He was unbending. Exasperated, she described the situation and her unhappiness to Betsy.

When Betsy filled me in on the details of the couple's negotiations thus far, she asked me what I thought our friend should do. I said that, it was a risk, but she should employ Boulwarism. Betsy asked me to define the term. I did, and our two great minds came to the same conclusion: the risk should be taken. The woman had really had it. She talked about leaving him. She was very much in love with him, but none of her concerns, arguments, or unhappiness seemed to move him. It was time for her to confront him.

My advice through Betsy was, "What did she have to lose?" If confronting him and refusing to negotiate—Boulwarism—didn't persuade him, then this tortured relationship would go on for years.

Our friend was more than ready. If she failed, she definitely wanted out. With my usual lack of humility, I assured Betsy it was a winner. Because of her seriousness, because he loved her, Boulwarism would work. It did. They're living happily ever after.

In general, Boulwarism can be used only when you have the power position. My friend's growing frustration gave her strength and reversed the power in her favor.

OTHER FACTORS THAT AFFECT CONFRONTATION

There are times when negotiations are settled by accident. There may be circumstances beyond your knowledge and control that dictate the outcome. Your lack of awareness of these circumstances may lead you to decide to avoid confrontation, especially if you believe the cards are stacked against you from the start. In the following example, a friend's perception of the circumstances, or rather misconception of them, led to his victory.

Dr. Russell, a well-known dentist in Greenwich Village, had rented a professional office in the ground floor of an apartment building for a number of years. He worked with one associate until his son decided to follow in his footsteps. Then there were three dentists working out of the office.

After twenty years of ownership, the landlord sold the building to overseas investors, who, of course, checked the rent roll to see how much the tenants were paying. The dentists' lease was coming up for renewal within the next year, and they and the new landlord were far apart in what each thought was a fair rent.

The negotiations were going nowhere. The dentists believed further talks to be futile, so they began to look for new space. While the sturm und drang continued, the original associate decided to retire. He notified Dr. Russell and began to pack his belongings. After the goodbyes, the moving van arrived and the movers began to load the associate's furniture and equipment.

The building superintendent, seeing the movers, rushed to the telephone to call the new owners. He said, excitedly, "The dentists are moving, the dentists are moving." He was aware of the new owners' desire to maintain the dentists as tenants.

Within the hour, a representative of one of the owners appeared at the dentists' office and ran up to the father and son dental team. "Where are you going? I'm sure we can work this out." The father and son realized what the owner thought and seized this moment of positive confrontation. They informed the owner that they had found new space, at a reasonable rent, but had not signed the lease yet. They said they would be willing to continue to negotiate for the existing space.

The dentists were now negotiating from a position of strength. It became clear that the new owners liked the prestige of having professional offices in the building. The dentists did not want to move. After a few more negotiating sessions, the deal was closed, very much in the dentists' favor.

Although the dentists did not intend for their move to be a tactic to inspire confrontation, it did, and the results were positive. In the following example, timing also altered the outcome. But in this case, poor timing exacerbated an already nonconfrontational negotiating style. Sadder still, it was not accidental, and the disastrous negotiations that followed could have been avoided.

Mayor David Dinkins selected as his chief negotiator a mediator named Eric Schmertz. Eric is a brilliant mediator and arbitrator. He could make for solutions that were ameliorative and productive for both sides. But negotiating was not his strong suit. He never denied this.

In his first negotiations with the unions, the mayor settled with the union that had the best argument. The United Federation of Teachers was led by a militant woman named Sandy Feldman. She had the facts supporting her demands. The school system in New York provided the teachers a painful working environment. Their compensation fell behind that of their colleagues in the suburban areas. Lower wages and poorer working conditions led to a high turnover rate. So Dinkins gave the teachers a fair settlement, one that he could not justify for the other unions whose contracts were yet to be negotiated. But this wage increase for the teachers set the pattern for the other unions, a pattern that New York City could not afford.

The press excoriated the mayor. The other unions were unhappy. The mayor and his negotiators should have delayed the most difficult and politically dangerous negotiations with the teachers' union. Subsequent events proved that it was one of the reasons he failed in his reelection bid.

The Dinkins administration was basically nonconfrontational. David set the tone. Bill Lynch, his chief deputy mayor, was a willing contributor in holding back. Eric Schmertz was more the mediator type and could not call tough shots. In this instance, nonconfrontation was counterproductive—not because the settlement was unfair but because the timing was disastrous.

My wife, Betsy, comes from a family where confrontation was despised. The silence was deafening. Betsy almost never heard her mother and father argue, and yet she was terribly affected by an unhappy marriage. Even as a child she wanted to see some action. She would have loved to see them talk it out, put it on the table, get their points across. This never happened. These long periods of silence meant that there would be no resolution to the difficulty in that family. As a result of never experiencing it, confrontation is frightening to her. She wants *civilized* confrontation. She would like confrontation to be low-key and disagreements to be discussed intelligently and reasonably, and without unpleasantness.

This kind of approach isn't my best card. For me, confrontation is more agitated—a little loud and a little aggressive. This would always upset Betsy. Her response would be, "My God, can't you lower your voice and let's talk it over." The compromise for me was to lower my voice. I had to recognize that for positive discussions to take place, it was most important for the woman I loved to hear my views with an even, level tone of voice. This adjustment on my part that Betsy regarded as a "civilized manner" allowed us to move in a more positive direction. We get a solution and we get therapy in terms of the problem itself. Since we have been together for only twenty-three years, I still have a way to go . . .

Arriving at a solution often requires compromise and flexibility. Nevertheless, it is almost impossible to go through a negotiation without airing some difficulties and confronting your adversary. Certainly you must understand and assess your adversary. In negotiating for some African art, my friend Lester Wunderman, an entrepreneur with an artistic eye, started from a confrontational base. The solution, however, was nonconfrontational.

Lester had a good relationship with this particular art dealer, but he always kept his guard up high, being suspicious of art dealers in general. The dealer showed Lester an excellent piece of sculpture. Lester wanted it, but not at the price the dealer was asking. The price was fair, but Lester did not want to spend that much. Negotiations came to a dead stop. Both sides had virtue and truth on their side. The negotiations were becoming confrontational.

Then Lester remembered that the art dealer was attracted to his Borgward Isabella, a fairly rare car that he owned. It was worth less than the price the dealer demanded for the piece of art. The negotiations for the price of the art had taken weeks. But when Lester bartered the car for the art, it was over in an hour.

Switching to another medium of exchange satisfied both sides. This tactic altered the confrontational nature of the talks and allowed the negotiations to proceed and, ultimately, be concluded to both sides' satisfaction. The art dealer received the car he always wanted, and Lester received a piece of art within his price range. Both triumphed. I'm not sure who got the better deal in this negotiation since I've never seen a Borgward Isabella. The important thing is that they both got what they wanted for what they were willing to pay, a perfect example of what can happen when you properly assess your adversary.

Chapter Three

THE STAKEHOLDERS IN THE NEGOTIATIONS

You are never alone in a negotiation. Even personal negotiations, which are often described as one-on-one, rarely concern only the two parties sitting at the bargaining table. Rather, they include everyone with a stake in the outcome. They may not be physically present, but they are there: the children in a divorce, the stockholders in a corporate merger, the members of the union you lead, the taxpayers who support the public agency you're part of. And there are the adversaries too: those on the other side of the table and those whom they represent.

Appraising your allies and your adversaries and the needs of each is an essential step in preparing for the talks. Like lawyers, negotiators represent their clients. Their mission is to meet clients' needs, not their own. In certain instances, particularly in major contract talks, there may even be competing needs among clients, a situation that requires double negotiations. First you get your own house in order; then you focus on your adversary. Similarly, your adversary's team may not be unified. It is useful to be aware of this information and use it to advantage during the talks.

Even when you are representing yourself in a negotiation, your own needs require careful analysis. What is your true bottom line? Are your goals short or long term? Are they realistic? Are they productive in the long run?

Whom Do You Represent, and What Are the Needs?

One of the best negotiators I know is Ted Ashley, television agent to the stars. His main strength as a negotiator is his ability to cut through the nonsense and get to the heart of his clients' needs. He then develops a strategy to meet those needs.

Ted was Carol Burnett's agent at the height of her television career. He had an extremely lucrative contract with Burnett, receiving 10 percent of all her earnings plus 10 percent of the costs of the production. Carol was signed with CBS, and Ted liked the stability it gave her career. It was a mutually beneficial arrangement.

Some difficulties developed when Carol's manager began talks with NBC, which had made her an excellent offer: for performing two specials a year, NBC would pay a very handsome salary. The offer suited her, and a meeting was arranged with her, her husband, her advisers, and Ted Ashley.

Ted was in a difficult position. He had to get CBS to top the offer, and substantially. These could not be nickel-and-dime negotiations.

Prior to the meeting, Ted spoke to James T. Aubrey of CBS, CEO Bill Paley's top lieutenant. Carol's current contract with CBS gave the studio an option to continue the terms of the agreement. Ted suggested CBS make two major concessions: give Burnett the continuity rights in the contract, and provide compensation to match or exceed that of the highest-paid female series star in a one-hour special.

Aubrey took Ted's proposal to Paley. He thought it was going to be a tough sell, but Paley embraced the package. Meanwhile, Ted's meeting with Burnett and her group was in progress. Ted knew the negotiations would go through the night and asked Aubrey to be available by telephone. Ted knew Carol and the others would want confirmation directly from CBS. He was right.

After Ted described the details of CBS's offer, Carol and her team said they wanted to hear it from Aubrey. A conference call with Aubrey at 4:00 A.M. confirmed the agreement. CBS and Ted kept the account.

Ashley's knowledge of the industry's protocol was an important element in reaching agreement. The key factor, however, was his understanding of his client's material needs, as well as his client's need to participate in the negotiations. Bringing Burnett in had made the difference.

Collective Needs

In a house purchase the person who's negotiating has to understand and consider the collective needs of all of those who will live in the house. One common mistake parents make is excluding the children from the discussion. Parents define the children's needs from their own perspective. Yet it's easy to talk to the kids and find out from them what they would like. Even if their requests appear to be outlandish or foolish, the parents will be better prepared to choose the right house for the family if they consider the children's needs.

Since I preceded my family in moving from Chicago to New York, my wife, Sarah, put the burden of finding a house on my shoulders. She gave me specific criteria to follow:

- It must be in suburbia.
- The town must have an excellent education system.
- The area must be quiet and safe.
- The size and design must accommodate all members of the family.

The financial details were my responsibility. Thanks to a magnificent real estate agent, I found a house that fit Sarah's description—or so I thought. It was in suburbia, across the street from a golf course, in a quiet and safe area. The house was a lovely Tudor with the requisite number of rooms. The education system in the town was considered adequate. And without any need to negotiate, the price was right.

We did not live there happily ever after.

After six months, Sarah pronounced the education system inadequate. My older children, Irving, age eleven, and Joshua, age fourteen, did not share this opinion. They were happy in their new school and loved their friends. But Sarah unilaterally decided to move, and she did so with great purpose and astonishing negotiating ability. She wanted to move to the town next to us, which had the superb school system she wanted.

She found an excellent house that met all of her criteria, except the price was not right. My contribution to the negotiations for the house was to say, "We can't afford it." Sarah, and the same magnificent realtor, resolved this by selling off a piece of the property to make the costs manageable.

Josh and Irv did not want to move. They were not asked, and they were unhappy. The move was not traumatic, but their unhappiness could have been avoided.

We moved. They made new friends. They grudgingly admitted the school was good, and the house was better. "Everybody has a room of their own," said Irv.

The move could have been much smoother if they had been included in the decision-making process. They would have realized sooner rather than later that Scarsdale was next door to White Plains, so they would not lose their good friends. It worked out, but they did resent the fact that their wishes and feelings were disregarded.

In our macho society, the responsibilities are usually broken down in two ways. In the purchase of a house, for example, the wife may define what she needs, and both husband and wife may decide on the cost and the financing. But the actual negotiations are usually left to the husband. This traditional division of duties is senseless and can be counterproductive. Strength as a negotiator has little to do with gender, but is instead a function of one's sensitivity, intelligence, and decision-making abilities.

The traditional breakdown—"she knows what she wants; he knows how to negotiate the costs"—is nonsense. The member of the family who has the greater understanding of the family's needs in a house is in the position to make a meaningful contribution to the negotiations. The member of the family who has the more intimate knowledge of the item can also be in a better position to understand the negotiations. That person should have strong input even if he or she doesn't do the negotiations.

Competing Needs

In major negotiations, you have to consider the specific needs of those you represent and often their specific competing needs. This is difficult and can be dangerous as well. The solution must be one that does not sacrifice one group's needs for those of another and thinks of the unity of the group as a whole.

When I arrived in New York, I was faced with a particular problem: District Council 37 of AFSCME had a large proportion of lower-income workers, but they did not have the right to collective bargaining. Therefore, they had not made the gains that the other groups within the union had, nor were their needs taken into consideration in any negotiations.

In 1966, we won a major election that gave the district council representation rights for the lower-income hospital workers and the clerks. Understandably, the leadership of these groups now held very high aspirations: we had won an underdog election, and I had proved my leadership by being a major winner.

To the victor belongs not only the spoils but the headaches.

Before my first negotiations, I looked at the numbers and the percentage increase available to us and realized that in all probability, we could hit a $6,000 minimum annual salary for low-income union members, which would give large increases to the poorest of our members. The percentages would be dramatic indeed. The challenge was to work out the deal without upsetting the mid-level and higher-paid membership. When I informed Herb Haber, the city's chief negotiator at the time, that I was going for a $6,000 minimum, he looked at me as though I was out of my mind, then assured me it wasn't feasible. I assured him that it was. We could do it by backloading and looking at the exact numbers—the dollars rather than the percentages. Even if the lower-income workers were to get a large percentage increase, the dollars would not be that high. He was intrigued. We both agreed that we would talk about dollars.

My insistence on a $6,000 minimum garnered a great deal of publicity. My adversary, New York City mayor John Lindsay, was sympathetic to raising the wages of lower-income workers; he genuinely believed in helping those who needed it the most. It got him into lots of trouble politically, but for me he was an absolute Godsend. We looked at the numbers, prepared all the arguments, and began to work it out. My research assistant, a man named Daniel Nelson, whom I stole from the Ladies Garment Workers Union, had an ability to manipulate numbers that was nothing short of genius. We worked on the package, and a contract was negotiated. The *Daily News* headlined it: CITY AGREES TO 6G PAY MINI-MUM.

We worked it out because we were prepared. We understood the inequities the hospital workers and clerks had experienced, and we understood that we could not have settled at the expense of the higher-paid workers. Traditional negotiations would have made the lower-income workers' settlement a pattern setter for all. We knew this was not realistic and settled on a strategy of bargaining separately for the lower-income workers. The negotiations were necessarily bifurcated. We negotiated for the lower-paid workers only after we reached a settlement for the higher-paid workers.

Another negotiation involving preparation for competing needs called for a very different strategy. The heavy-duty motor vehicle operators did some of the most difficult tasks among all of the motor vehicle operators (MVOs). They drove heavy truckloads, operated forklifts and cranes, and did some of the toughest and dirtiest work in the city. These operators were traditionally the younger drivers with the least seniority. The chauffeurs and light vehicle drivers were the old-timers, and they controlled the situation. It was blatantly unfair, and I felt strongly that it should be corrected. I took on the cause of the MVOs and managed to negotiate an extra percentage increase for the heavy-duty MVOs even though it was at the expense of the chauffeurs. It was a hard sell, but I explained to the old-timers that we owed it to the next generation of workers to discontinue the inherent inequities in pay, considering the difficult job the MVOs performed. In the end, the contract was ratified. The specific needs of the MVOs won out.

When you face a situation of competing needs, preparation in understanding the specific needs of the people you represent is key. I not only worked at it; I had a staff of representatives who were extremely sensitive to the members and always kept their ears to the ground. In addition, I had Lillian Roberts, one of the best trade unionists in terms of her knowledge of the rank and file. I owe much to Lillian and the incredibly proficient staff who helped me prepare.

The Client Comes First

In negotiations, you must never lose sight of the fact that the needs of those you represent are paramount. Here's an example of how differences between the negotiator and his client played out.

My son Irv was representing a young woman in contract negotiations with her employer, a major New York newspaper. The woman was considered a valued employee. Her goals in the negotiations, however, were tempered by her awareness of her employer's financial problems, which restricted its ability to raise wages, and her long-range ambitions. She did not want to stay with the paper for more than two more years.

The woman's goals were rather modest, but as her representative, my son wanted a decent wage settlement. In discussing the situation with him, I reminded him that a negotiator does not represent himself. He had to define the situation in terms of his client's needs. Recognizing this, he developed a strategy based on the woman's acknowledged abilities. He could not play it hard, because she didn't want to play it hard. There is often an inclination by negotiators to score high, but it makes little sense when those who are being represented have a more modest goal.

In the ensuing negotiations, management was polite but distant. Irv discussed the situation with his client, and she was not the least bit perturbed. His goal was to reach the high point of her low level of aspiration, a situation that did not call for toughing it out. The young woman was prepared to find another position, and management risked losing a valued employee.

The woman Irv represented accepted management's final offer. My son would have loved to have negotiated a greater salary increase for his client, but he had to abide by her wishes, not his own—and he gained good experience.

Determining the Real Needs

A good negotiator will not take his clients' initial goals as cast in stone. They may think they need one thing. Sometimes they do, but sometimes they really need another. When the client is not on target, the negotiator must steer the person in a different direction for the client's sake. For personal negotiations where emotions are high, the negotiator often defines or redefines the client's needs. The negotiator becomes a therapist in a sense. In the following example, shock therapy was called for.

A close friend had a terrible marriage, and a breakup was inevitable. It was embarrassing to be in their company. They either tore into each other or indulged themselves in a dreadful silence. And then he had an open affair with a younger woman. They were seen together everywhere, and he could not care less.

Our friend isolated herself. She stopped eating and refused to get help. She was even bordering on suicidal.

We all took turns trying to shake her out of it. We had been trying to be sensitive, but to no avail, so I told Betsy, who was now very worried, that I'd like to try another approach. I turned to insensitivity, vulgarity, and shock negotiations.

Betsy and I visited her, and I went into a dramatic monologue: "You and Harvey couldn't stand each other. You are wrapping yourself in pity when you ought to be breathing a sigh of relief that it's over. The bastard is zinging you with an open affair. You ought to be thankful. He's given you the opening. Get the hell out of it."

For the first time she listened. I then suggested we go for dinner—actually, more than "suggested." "Mildred, if you don't join us for dinner, I'll drag you there."

She left for dinner with us. Then Betsy took over and point by point let her know how fortunate she was. Initially silent, Mildred soon realized that her need to reunite with her husband was misguided and foolish at best. What she really needed was to work on a plan to get on with her life.

Time healed the wound. I don't know how Harvey is doing, but Mildred is now in great shape.

When Betsy and I decided to move to Manhattan, I insisted we needed a house, not an apartment. In my mind, we were leaving our Brooklyn brownstone, which met our needs, and were simply replacing it in another location.

After seeing several houses, we found what we believed to be perfect for us—a gorgeous brownstone with a backyard for entertaining and for Sophie, our dog. We called on an architect friend to assess the condition of the house, as well as its aesthetics. Her assistance, however, took another form.

She loved the house. It was magnificent and impeccably maintained, requiring only minor interior renovation to meet our needs. This four-story brownstone provided more than ample space for us. My friend, however, had a reservation. Although we would occupy only three of the four floors, two of the floors had mezzanines which, in effect, meant living vertically on five floors.

She kept looking at the stairs and finally said, "Victor, you're seventy-five years old. I know you are going to live forever, but look at all of these stairs!" She then asked, "Why do you need all of this space? You do most of your entertaining in Bellport [our weekend and summer home]. A large apartment would more than satisfy your space needs."

She was right. I was hung up on moving to a house. It somehow made the transition from Brooklyn easier. All along, Betsy believed we should be looking for an apartment, but she was respecting my wishes since I had had difficulty with the decision to move from Brooklyn in the first place.

Betsy and I changed course and started looking at apartments. It has been almost two years since we moved to our apartment at the Beresford on Central Park West. It's perfect for us, and Betsy walks to work.

WHO ARE YOUR ADVERSARIES, AND WHAT ARE THEIR NEEDS?

Although understanding the goals and needs of your allies and your own membership is paramount, it is as important, though much more difficult, to gain these same insights into the people on the other side of the table—your adversaries. However difficult, you must learn everything you can about the players and their positions on the issues. For public figures, information may be readily available in the press. For personal negotiations, where the participants are private citizens, you may have to dig deeper. What is the reputation of your real estate agent or your wife's divorce lawyer? Who are their former clients, and what were the outcomes of previous negotiations? How long have they been in business? The most important thing is to avoid painting everyone with the same brush. Everyone is an individual, and you should prepare for each situation.

Every Adversary Is Unique

There was tremendous variation among the mayors I dealt with, and an even greater variation among their negotiating teams.

The first mayor with whom I negotiated was Robert Wagner, an intelligent and fair man. He took office when the collective bargaining process was new; we really hadn't reached full sophistication in regard to either the negotiating process or the negotiations outcome, and most of the settlements were handled quietly in the drawing room of Gracie Mansion or in the office of Harry Bronstein, the mayor's budget director. Bronstein was an old-time civil servant who was respected by those who dealt with him. For a while it suited everybody. But it was bound to erode.

The parameters of negotiations were not well defined in this early period of collective bargaining, leaving the strike as a primary negotiating tactic. It took a strike to bring about the health plan system for public employees and another to bring about impartial third-party dispute settlements. This was not the fault of any one person—the mayor or Bronstein or myself. Indeed, it was a necessary transition that was taking place in the public sector. I sometimes think that Robert Wagner was similar to Gorbachev. He started the revolution in collective bargaining, but others had to complete the process.

The times and the personalities of the mayors made for different kinds of needs and negotiations. Bob Wagner was sophisticated, quiet, and intelligent and had the deserved respect of most of the major labor leaders. He fit in perfectly with the time.

Abe Beame was so much a part of New York's fiscal crisis that it is impossible to discuss him adequately here. I will only note that he was probably the most decent man I ever knew. Abe did not have a bad bone in his body.

Ed Koch, irascible and tough, loved a fight. He fit with my own personality, and we would debate the issues. If either one of us backed down, we would look terribly weak. I couldn't let him get away with his one-liners and his periodic nastiness. I had to match them.

His negotiating team was excellent and was totally aware of the byplay between us. In the beginning of the Koch administration, Basil Paterson, a dignified and sensitive gentleman, had hoped that we would both slow down and, in fact, let Ed Koch know this. It was well meaning but futile, and to Basil's credit he worked effectively within the situation. He was an excellent negotiator and let the storm swirl around him while he got down to business.

It is interesting that Koch selected dignified, quiet labor relations experts, such as Basil and, later, people like Bruce McIver and Ed Silver—fair, intelligent, and wonderful to work with. So behind-the-scenes-negotiations were quiet, progressive and skillfully handled. The outcome benefited both Koch and myself, and the city.

Wagner and Koch had different personalities, different styles of negotiating, and different needs as dictated by the economic and political climates in which they served. Nevertheless, with both, we could settle on an agreement that would benefit all concerned, especially if I did my homework and knew what to expect before the talks began.

When a mayor is new, there is always an orientation and transition period. I had to learn about each one and the people they brought in. Of course, the mayor's background, reputation, and errors of omission and commission are a matter of public record. The mayor's professional staff, however, is a different, and more difficult, matter. I had to try to find people who knew them and get an idea of their background. This detective work is essential. The time spent researching the players will save time, and trouble, in the long run. The more you know about your adversaries, the better your preparation and ability to negotiate will be.

I deliberately skipped over one mayor with whom I negotiated. Lindsay was an enigma. At the beginning of his term, I would ask myself from time to time, "Is he for real?" He seemed to have no comprehension of negotiations. In fact, he had a disdain for negotiations. Even more regrettable, he had few, if any, experienced negotiators on his staff.

I needed a viable Mayor Lindsay. I had to prepare for his weaknesses to keep him from making mistakes. We were both new and had to be supportive of each other. My assistance to Lindsay came in the form of support during some of his major labor crises, such as the "education wars" fought with the powerful head of the teachers' union, Al Shanker, beginning in 1968. Although the vast majority of the labor movement opposed Lindsay's reelection in 1969, DC 37 endorsed him.

We worked together beautifully. I got to know him and found a decent, idealistic human being, who was politically accident prone.

Identifying the Decision-Maker

In major negotiations with the city, the stakes are high. In most cases, the mayor is not the chief negotiator; however, he is the chief policy-maker, so it's important to know how much policy flexibility he gives to his chief negotiator. It is a given that the mayor will make the final decision, but he stays behind the scenes and will allow his chief negotiator some policy flexibility.

In corporate mergers or other business negotiations, it can be the chief financial officer who carries substantial weight. Or it may be somebody else within the CEO's office. If not the chief financial officer, it may be the general counsel or the CEO. You need to find out who is the real power.

A close friend of mine, a woman with excellent ability, had to negotiate a merger with a major corporation. She represented a small company. During the talks, a top executive of the larger organization showed up with a staff of twenty. He launched into his litany of demands, including absorbing two of her company's main products into his product lines. She knew the results of his proposition would be devastating to her company, but he wouldn't budge. This was a nonnegotiable item for him.

As the negotiations continued, he was as rigid on every other issue as on the first. He believed that any give on his part would make him lose face. The fact that his adversary was a diminutive woman probably compounded his desire to be unyielding. She was convinced she had a losing negotiation and ended the negotiations with the executive.

Up against a wall, she rolled the dice and went over his head. Her instincts about his inability to negotiate, coupled with her understanding of the needs of her own company and the larger organization, paid off. The CEO of the larger company, a sensitive and reasonable man, consummated the deal. She made a dangerous gamble, but it worked because she knew she had nothing to lose by going to the final decision-maker.

Winning Your Adversaries' Trust

A friend was called in to mediate when talks between the NBC Network News Department and the new General Electric management of NBC broke down. His was not the usual role of the mediator. In this case, the expectation was that he would come up with a negotiated solution.

In order to resolve the difficulties, it was imperative that he fully analyze and understand the issues and the players on both sides. The issues, it turned out, were fairly standard, but they were magnified by the sheer size of both NBC and GE and by the fact that the NBC staff and GE management did not trust each other.

The Network News Department believed that news was a public service. The economics of the situation were of small moment to them. They regarded the new GE owners as interlopers, concerned only with the bottom line.

GE insisted that they shared the belief that news was a public service. They were concerned, however, that the news department was suffering what they said was a $100 million annual loss. GE as a whole could absorb such a loss, but, the NBC component of GE was valued at $300 million. A $100 million loss was a staggering figure under this valuation.

The new GE management compounded the problem with a terribly counterproductive mistake: they asked that Network News make a contribution to GE's Political Action Campaign Fund. The negotiators for GE said they were making this request to boost the news staffs' position in the eyes of the GE hierarchy. The request left the Network News staff feeling that their worst fears were confirmed.

My friend believed the way to deal with the mistrust and resulting lack of cooperation by the Network News staff was through education. He argued that the failing finances of Network News were counterproductive for the staff. He set up a group of twenty-four from Network News, and through discussion they learned how the existing economic situation rewarded the least productive workers.

Compensation had not been based on merit. Some of the best people, including a top reporter, were being shortchanged. Through a frank discussion of the facts, this group of twenty-four was able to recognize the role of economics through self-education. They disseminated the information within the news group and demonstrated how counterproductive the situation had become. They had gotten beyond their instinctive attitude of mistrust and were now focused on the facts. My friend made certain the staff of NBC arrived at an educated conclusion.

Movement on the part of the professionals in Network News then took place. The role of my friend was now to talk to the new GE leadership. As the Network News people began to recognize that good professionalism and good economy go hand in hand, the GE management began to respect the professionalism and quality of the Network News people. Both groups then moved toward each other. The solution was a positive one based on excellent preparation and analysis.

One of the most difficult adversaries a negotiator can encounter is the community. City planners, developers, builders, and architects have all seen worthwhile projects die a slow death in the public approval process. Even projects that do not officially require public approval are left on the drawing boards unless a careful, thorough, sensitive approach is taken by the negotiator. Understanding the needs of a community and respecting those needs can turn even the fiercest adversaries into partners.

With some seed money from the New York Times Neediest Cases Fund, David Jones, head of the nonprofit Community Service Society (CSS), embarked on a plan to rehabilitate one thousand apartment units in a two-block area in the South Bronx in dire need of development.

Although Jones and his father were well known and respected in the neighborhood, the residents were fearful of being uprooted. The community was without an anchoring community-based organization and was not terribly unified or activist in nature. On the surface this might appear to be a plus, but it meant there was no established leadership for the tenants to turn to for guidance or anyone with whom the CSS could negotiate. The need for housing was apparent, but the residents were suspicious.

Jones realized he needed to gain their trust. He knew that in order to do so, he would need to develop a leadership body within the community with which he could negotiate. He needed people on the opposite side of the table who had the respect of the community and could make a deal stick. Jones worked with the community to identify its own leadership. The negotiations could now begin.

Jones and the new leadership selected one house to pilot their program. The tenants there were more secure with change and were ready to move—so an early win would be easy. Those representing the community had the respect of the tenants since David did not hand-pick them. But although the new leaders were respected and the majority of the tenants were on board, David knew the situation could not be rushed. The negotiations took months. Painstaking care was required in building trust by assuring the tenants that they would not be arbitrarily uprooted. As the tenants in the pilot building affirmed CSS's plans, the domino effect occurred, and the tenants of the other buildings joined in. A consonance of interest was created at the bargaining table, one built on trust.

Chapter Four

THE CONTEXT OF THE TALKS

Once you have an understanding of your own and your adversary's negotiating style and the goals and the needs of your side, and perhaps also of your adversary, the next step is to understand the context of the talks. Whether they're held at the bargaining table or the kitchen table, the negotiations cannot be separated from the economic and political environments in which they take place. Other factors, such as timing, previous relationships, and relevant precedents, should also be considered in preparation for the talks.

Are you buying your first house during peak house-selling season? Is the neighborhood appreciating? Are interest rates rising or declining? The objective is to acquire the information before you commit yourself to a specific strategy and certainly before the negotiations begin. If you don't have a good understanding of the context of the talks, chances are that your strategy won't work.

The information you derive from your preparation is the only leverage you can plan on before the talks begin. At a minimum, you'll know what the odds are, for or against you, and if you do lose, you will be able to diminish the fallout. You can never be too prepared, and you can never have too many facts. These will always help you in the bargaining process.

Your preparation should include a thorough and objective appraisal of the overall economic and political environment in which you are negotiating. For negotiations of a personal nature, such as divorce or buying a house or a new car, your appraisal may be limited to your own situation. For major negotiations involving labor contracts or international business issues, the range of your preparation will expand to include macroeconomic and political factors. A thoughtful analysis of these issues will help you formulate your initial proposals and negotiating strategy.

The Economic and Political Environments

Throughout the years I presided over District Council 37, from the end of the Wagner administration through the Lindsay, Beame, and Koch administrations (up to 1985), the environment was generally conducive to bargaining. No matter how bad the fiscal numbers were, there was always a feeling that the city could borrow its way out. Everyone played the borrowing game.

This became evident when Mayor John Lindsay appealed to the New York State governor Nelson Rockefeller for the right to tax since he didn't want to continue borrowing to a point that was dangerous. The negotiations went badly. The governor, in a tight political situation himself, rejected any increases in taxes and insisted on further borrowing, so the city plugged its budget gap through loans.

A few years later, when Governor Rockefeller became Vice President Rockefeller, he chastised the city for its debt load and its borrowing. When Rockefeller was governor it was politically and economically feasible to continue to borrow. It was easy to absorb and nobody was complaining—at least not complaining in a loud voice. So the borrowing went on.

The New York City fiscal crisis in 1975 changed that situation. Taxation replaced borrowing as a means of securing revenue. It was part of everybody's sharing the burden. Balancing of the books, balancing of the budget became signs of the times and the signs of the future.

Now there is a radical change in the use of taxation—a change of monumental consequence not only to unionized workers, but to society in general. Today, every politician wants to roll back taxes. This has led to a cutback in public funds, leading to cutbacks in services and in public sector jobs. It has also led to a restrictive negotiating environment in the public sector. Tax cuts reduce the amount of money available for negotiation, leaving workers with fewer benefits and fewer, if any, wage increases.

Unions find themselves in a far more difficult position today than during the 1975 fiscal crisis, when all parties could work their way out. The situation in the near future will mean sacrifice on the part of the poor and those who work for modest wages. Both the Census Bureau and the Bureau of Labor Statistics confirm that we are a society of the rich getting richer and the poor getting poorer. A society that fosters economic inequality is not sensitive to the needs of working people. This issue now comes to the forefront for anyone who must negotiate new labor-management agreements.

In a *New York Times* article of April 17, 1995, reporter Keith Bradsher quotes Professor Edward N. Wolff, an economist at New York University: "We are the most unequal industrialized society in terms of income and we are growing more unequal faster than the other industrialized countries." The major explanations for this inequality are:

- Falling wages for unskilled workers
- Decline of trade unions
- Technological changes
- Low tax rates on the rich

This must affect the collective bargaining scene. There is less money available and a greater share of profits is going to the already affluent. Upper management is generously compensated, while workers' salaries stand frozen or are minimally increased contractually. One can argue the unfairness of this in terms of our society, but the Democrats have gone along with it, while the Republicans relish it.

Working Within the Context

Understanding the economic and political context is key to developing a negotiating strategy and, ultimately, to finding solutions. However, there must also be a willingness by both parties to reach agreement. Often, previous relationships and performances or reputations become an important aspect of the context of the talks.

In the following example, despite a difficult economic and political situation, the two parties were willing to work within the given parameters and reach a positive agreement.

Harvey Weinstein was totally dedicated to New York City. A Brooklyn boy, he became CEO of Lord West, the only tuxedo manufacturer in the city. He employed four hundred unionized workers in a ninety-thousand-square-foot factory in the Chelsea section of the city.

In 1985, his lease was up for renewal, and the landlord informed him it would not be renewed. The neighborhood had become more residential, and the property had increased in value. The landlord intended to convert the factory to residential space.

This seemed to be the final straw for Weinstein's beleaguered business. Domestically, the garment industry had moved south to non-union shops. Globally, imports were making strong inroads in the textile and garment markets. But rather than give up, Harvey phoned Herb Brickman, one of Mayor Koch's top administrators, and asked for a meeting to negotiate some relief. Through Brickman, Koch assured him that "under no circumstances should Harvey think of leaving New York." While Harvey identified with Koch and wanted to stay in New York, the economics were subverting him. His was a marginal industry, and he needed savings to run his business.

He prepared for the negotiations by analyzing the savings he could make by moving the company to New Jersey—at least 15 percent savings through decreased utility costs, lower taxes, and lower labor costs since new workers' salaries would be lower than the salaries of those who had worked with him over the years.

Koch brought in Alair Townsend, his deputy mayor for finance. Harvey focused the talks on his need for savings and also explained his desire to build and own a new production plant.

The Koch administration went all out. They assisted him in finding a site for a new plant in Queens and included tax incentives, moving expenses, utility savings, and loan guarantees in their package. Harvey achieved labor savings through productivity gains negotiated with the Amalgamated Clothing Workers.

Harvey and his dedication to New York became an important aspect of the context of the talks in this negotiation. The most important aspect in his negotiating a favorable outcome, however, was his thorough preparation. His factory still operates in Queens, employing four hundred unionized workers. (He also sold me a tuxedo wholesale.)

TIMING

Time pressures can become the overriding aspect of the context of the negotiations. This often occurs in real estate transactions. The need for haste, however, can make waste in any negotiation.

A close friend had an agreement that he and his wife would raise their friend's two children if anything happened to her. She was a single parent. When her children were fifteen and seventeen, she passed away after a brief illness, leaving my friends totally unprepared. They would now have to accommodate two adolescents in their two-bedroom apartment or find a new apartment. But they had recently invested $250,000 in renovating their apartment and didn't want to move.

The teenagers had been raised in upper-class fashion and were unenthusiastic about their new quarters. This change in lifestyle, coupled with the loss of their mother, did not make for a happy situation. My friends shared the children's unhappiness. Then there was good news: an apartment on the same floor as theirs was for sale.

The apartment's only entrance was via the service elevator, a drawback to most buyers that made the apartment difficult to sell. However, it was of no concern to my friends since they would combine the new apartment with their existing one and use the more convenient access that they already had. The apartment's drawback would have typically put my friends in a favored negotiating position, but their urgency obliterated their advantage. The adolescents were growing restless, and so time was not on my friends' side. The seller was in no hurry, further weakening my friends' negotiating stance.

My friends priced the apartment at $750,000. They had invested $250,000 in renovating their existing apartment. They figured that if they had to move elsewhere, renovation expenses would be required; so they realistically added the $250,000 to their assessment of the value of the adjacent apartment.

My friends offered $1 million for the apartment. The negotiations began, and the price reached $1.1 million. The seller seemed amenable, but my friends found it difficult to close. Then, much to their surprise, the elderly seller, feeling she was at a disadvantage negotiating with a man (the husband was the primary negotiator), insisted she negotiate with his wife. In negotiations, the adversary does not have the right to choose the opposing negotiator. But the woman in this situation had the power, and she had time. They didn't. My friends conceded.

The seller then ratcheted the cost up to $1.2 million. My friends reasoned in this way: "We knew the cost would be $1 million. We'll save the $250,000 we've already invested in our apartment by staying in it and incorporating this new one. Moving could be disastrous. The kids should not be uprooted again. Once we combine the apartments, our quarters will be perfect. Besides, we can afford it."

The seller did not have to negotiate. By holding tight, her power grew. The longer it took, the more desperate my friends would become. My friends realized the price could go up even more, and they cut the deal. It worked out very well considering the context. The adolescents are happy—as happy as adolescents can be.

THE GLOBAL CONTEXT

Earlier I described the problems of Sol "Chick" Chaikin, then president of the International Ladies Garment Workers Union. His members' industry was disappearing, moving overseas where wages were impossibly low.

Macroeconomic factors can cut your ability to bargain. Under no circumstances can you ignore the compelling negative effects of the total marketplace—including the international market. These factors put labor negotiations on the defensive. Worse, you have little control over your diminished ability to negotiate decent work standards and wage conditions for your members.

International negotiations are even more difficult. In negotiations between nations, the parameters become wider and more distorted, and the problems are compounded. The political aspects of the situation can be even more inhibiting to the negotiators. Everybody may know what is wrong, but to speak out publicly can be counterproductive.

In the Israeli-Arab peace process, there are two groups that aren't at the table but are the most inhibiting factors in making progress. The Arab extremists, who don't want a peace pact at all, are more active than ever. On the Israeli side, the right-wing hardliners take advantage of any activity carried out by the Arab extremists. This makes it almost impossible to advance on the peace negotiations. There are continual breakdowns after each Arab extremist activity. Negotiating in that environment where the Israeli and Arab extremes feed on each other is filled with pitfalls.

Prime Minister Yitzhak Rabin of Israel tried to advance the

peace process by agreeing to relinquish Israeli territory for a peace commitment from the Palestine Liberation Organization (PLO). He was assassinated by a right-wing Israeli fanatic.

Rabin's successor, Shimon Peres, also tried to advance the peace process. He was undone by suicide bombings in Israel committed by Hamas, a right-wing Palestinian guerrilla organization opposed to the mainstream PLO. As a consequence, Peres was defeated by Benjamin Netanyahu, who wanted to slow the peace process. Additional Hamas-sponsored suicide bombings brought the peace process to a complete halt. As of the writing of this book, the United States is trying desperately to revive the peace talks, but the right-wingers on both sides seem to be succeeding in what they want: continued hostilities between Israel and the PLO. Most recently, there seems to be a softening on the part of Netanyahu. In situations as volatile as this, it is risky to make predictions. Netanyahu may surprise us. I believe he is a hawk who would like to take on the wings of a dove.

The environmental factors—in this case, political factors—have a direct bearing on the efforts toward a negotiated settlement. No negotiations are free from the environment in which they occur. It is imperative that you recognize the strengths, weaknesses, and trustworthy characteristics of your adversary. The Israels have no choice but to negotiate with Yasir Arafat, president of the PLO, a man they do not like. Likewise, as much as Arafat hates the Israelis, it is they with whom he must come to terms, and he can do this only by negotiating with them.

In any kind of negotiations, it is counterproductive to insist on a change in your adversary's chief negotiator. The Israeli insistence over the years that they would not deal with the PLO actually strengthened Arafat's hand. Israel helped make him the most important and popular Arab leader. Only when they agreed to negotiate with him was there a possibility of a negotiated peace.

Trying to remove your major adversary unnecessarily complicates future relationships whether the adversary is the prime minister, the union's chief negotiator, your ex-husband, or the seller of the home you hope to purchase.

But Environment Isn't Everything

Environment is certainly an important factor in any negotiation, but other factors also count. Sometimes circumstances peculiar to the individuals or the situation far outweigh the negotiating environment. Here is another example from my personal real estate history that illustrates this point.

In 1975, Betsy and I rented our brownstone apartment in Brooklyn Heights. The neighborhood was a quiet contrast to the hectic activity of our business and social life, and we loved it. Above all we loved the apartment and the house it was in. Then we started to worry. The owner was an absentee landlord, and we feared that he'd sell the house from under us. Our only assurance to staying in this spot would be to buy the house.

Although we had no idea whether the house was for sale, we phoned the owner and made an offer. We started at a low $165,000 and let him know that we were interested in buying. No dice—he wasn't selling. I asked if he thought the price was too low. "No, Victor. I'm not selling at any price."

Sometime after, he called me because he had a terrible problem. He was a sculptor and was planning an exhibit of his work. Unfortunately, most of his sculptures were locked in the hold of a ship, and the longshoremen were on strike. Almost hysterical, he wanted to know if I could be of any help. I could. I knew the strike was almost over, and it would not be very difficult for me to do as he asked. I got in touch with the longshoremen leadership, who assured me it would be easy. Just get them the bill of lading and the deed was done. My landlord received his sculptures, and the show was able to go on.

A few months later, he phoned and told me that he and his wife would be delighted to sell the house to us. They didn't want to sell but there was no reason for them to keep it, and they would love for Betsy and me to bid on the house. We agreed to meet for brunch about a week later, and I immediately went to work on preparing for the negotiations.

I went to my associate Ralph Pepe. He told me that the house was probably worth about $250,000, which I really couldn't afford. If I went to $225,000, I initially thought I would be house poor, but after reviewing our financial situation, Betsy, Ralph, and I figured we could go this high. My income would be increasing, and the house was in an appreciating neighborhood. The other neighborhoods in that area, Boerum Hill and Cobble Hill, were also appreciating.

The negotiations started during brunch with the owner's asking us what we were willing to pay. I started off almost apologetically by restating our original offer of $165,000. I explained that Betsy and I were financially tight since I was involved in a divorce and we had just moved in together. He stopped me in mid-sentence, looked at his wife, and said, "I think $165,000 is fair." She smiled and nodded.

I then told him I needed a second mortgage of $50,000. Ralph had mentioned to me that 10 percent interest would have been fair. The seller asked me what percentage I was paying for my first mortgage and I told him 7.5 percent. He turned to his wife again and said, "That really is all we get on our investments anyway. I think this makes sense. Victor, let's call it a deal, but I must ask one thing of you. Just let the lawyers put it in legal language, and we have an agreement." We shook hands on the agreement, and I shook them rather fast.

The sellers were not unprepared. Their social and economic circumstances allowed them to be generous, and so they were. They were fairly well off, they wanted to be gracious, and the material cost to them was minimal. The savings to Betsy and myself were monumental.

My preparations had been meaningful. They gave Betsy and me security. Ralph's concerns about how much we could pay and what kind of mortgage we could carry helped us prepare. As it turned out, we didn't need to call on all our resources, but the preparations were still enormously helpful.

Preparation is always necessary. Sometimes you get breaks; however, the breaks could fall the other way, as they did with my friends who were buying the apartment. But the personalities and the different needs of the negotiators are always crucial in every negotiation.

If the sellers really wanted to drive a bargain, it's just as well that I came prepared. They weren't. They were generous, and I was fortunate. Environment is important, but it isn't everything.

CONTEXT IN THE WORKPLACE

In the workplace, employee relations and negotiations with a boss or supervisor occur in an inherently hierarchical environment. The context of the talks depends on one's position within the organization or company, and all too often the employee or job applicant approaches the negotiations from a position of weakness (a strong reason for joining a union). This understandable and sometimes self-inflicted feeling of weakness is detrimental to successful negotiations. It can be overcome even by novice negotiators. To begin, one's position within an organization does not define the entire context. Is the company making a profit? Is it expanding or downsizing? How long have you been employed there? What is the status of your department? These are but a few of the questions you should address to assess the environment in which you will be negotiating a raise or promotion. Most important, you should objectively assess your own individual value to the organization. This information will help you to diminish any feeling of weakness you may have in approaching the negotiations and enable you to communicate your worth to your employer better during the talks.

A top staffer in the union wanted an increase. She was in a fairly good negotiating position since I needed her. Her performance was excellent, and she made a great contribution to the union. She was a department head, and her salary was consistent with those of her counterparts.

This was a tough negotiation. The union at that time had a restricted budget. There was no way I could raise her salary without raising the other department heads' salaries as well. There would be a domino effect. In negotiations, you evaluate the pluses and the minuses. Giving her an increase could be too costly. I decided to hold firm. My negotiating card was to give her assurances for the future. I sincerely believed the budget would loosen up.

This is another aspect of negotiations. You don't kid yourself. I never recommend dishonesty. You can hold back on some facts, but never distort the facts. My recommendation was for her to look to the future, and it worked out. Less than a year later, I was able to raise her salary along with those of the other top administrators.

The chief negotiator must decide on the bottom line. You set the parameters. It may not work, but only you can make the evaluation. I decided that losing her would be less onerous than a major budgetary deficit for the union. Fortunately, she stayed.

Determining your worth—how you fit in or do not fit into an employment situation—is not always easy. You may need an objective opinion in evaluating yourself and developing a strategy when negotiating for a raise or other change in your job status.

A friend of mine was in this type of situation and asked for my assistance. He was a top fiscal officer in a major organization and was holding all the cards—except one: confidence. He was a bundle of nerves, and this was clearly negating his excellent negotiating position.

My friend was being offered a new contract by a rival company. It gave him all of the security and benefits that he didn't have in his current job. But the organization he was contemplating leaving was very powerful in his field, and he feared retaliation for leaving. He poured out his anxiety to me: "They could hurt my career. They could make erroneous accusations. They could force me to stay."

My question to him was simple and compelling: "How can they do this?"

They couldn't. In fact, they wouldn't, for the same reasons they wanted him to remain with the company. They had no hostility toward him. The situation and the economic environment was in his favor, yet his lack of negotiating experience made him a nervous wreck.

My advice was almost unnecessary: "Just do it." He was in the catbird seat. I still had to address his specific fears, so I responded to his questions.

Q.What if they try to disparage my abilities?

A.It's your ability that brought about the offer for the new position. Would it really affect your new company? Obviously not.

Q.What if they harangue and insult me?

A.So what? You're leaving. You have a new position. In fact, the angrier they become, the more solidifying for you. And it will only prove that they really wanted you to stay.

Q.I do have a contractual relationship with them. Upon leaving, I cannot divulge any information about the firm. How can I defend myself against accusations that my old firm might make?

A.This is a legitimate and correct concern of theirs. You will carry out your obligations as long as there is a smooth transition. If they don't violate an agreement, then you don't violate an agreement.

His questions led me to believe he had nothing to worry about. The movement on his part was now pro forma: give them some notice; treat any severance entitlement as an established fact. Severance agreements can be eliminated if you quit, but it is not unusual for severance agreements to be honored if the employee agrees to give sufficient notice of his departure, particularly if the employee has been with the company a number of years. I also advised him not to be negative. He was a winner, and winners should be neither negative nor arrogant.

My friend was now prepared for his exit interview. It turned out that there were no pitfalls, and everybody wished each other well. His fears had been groundless.

The truth is that since he was a fiscal officer leaving the firm, the administration's hierarchy could have been concerned about retaliation on *his* part. He breathed a sigh of relief, but so did the people in his former firm.

We then moved to the new business of the day, discussing his new contract. The man was an attractive prospect for the new company. His negotiations with the new firm were easier and more positive than those involving his departure. My son Irv did a magnificent job of negotiating his new contract. Irv understood that my friend and the new company both wanted to make it work. Most important, Irv understood the economic and political realities facing the new firm. The climate was right. My friend is doing well, and will continue to do better.

EVERYDAY CONTEXT

Even in the most mundane, routine transactions, knowledge of the context can give you the leverage you need for positive results. For the consumer, the supply and demand rule generally dictates prices and ability to negotiate for a lower cost. In the following example, the context was determined by the weather and a friend's understanding of how it could affect a deal.

Wandering around a country antique shop known for its high prices and nonbargaining stance, my friend spotted the perfect loveseat she was seeking. It was a cold, rainy January day, and the temperature was rapidly dropping. Few had dared to negotiate the icy road conditions; she was the store's sole customer.

After eyeing the loveseat and its price tag, my friend spent about a half-hour looking at the other antiques for sale and finally asked the shopkeeper if she had any other loveseats. When she was told there was only one, my friend said, "I was really looking for something a little more substantial. The loveseat is pretty, but I'm not sure it will work well in my parlor. I'll just take this" (a twelve dollar item she liked).

While she was paying for the small item, she casually asked if the price of the loveseat could be reduced, stressing that it was not exactly what she wanted. The saleswoman said she'd have to check, and returned in minutes with a 25 percent reduction, as well as an offer to deliver it free of charge.

In this case, the weather determined the context. Being the only customer in the store afforded my friend an opportunity to negotiate that would have been out of the question on a typical day. It changed the context. She understood that and took advantage of it.

PART TWO

Special Topics on Negotiating

Chapter Five

PREPARING FOR MAJOR NEGOTIATIONS

To recap, the four basic principles in preparing for any negotiation, large or small, are:

- Look at yourself as a negotiator
- Look at your adversary's negotiating style and ability
- Evaluate the stakes and the need for the talks
- Understand the context of the talks

The extent to which you will use these principles varies in different negotiating scenarios. For example, in major negotiations, you may have numerous constituents and adversaries. In personal negotiations, there may be only one. Nevertheless, assessing your own and your adversary's negotiating style and ability are the initial steps of the negotiations process, whether large or small.

Your preparation isn't complete until you thoroughly understand the issues being negotiated and the context of the talks. In major negotiations, the preparation required can sometimes seem overwhelming. In negotiating a single item, usually a mistake can be rectified, even forgiven, because it involves a small group—perhaps your family, perhaps only yourself. In major negotiations, whether corporate or union, the stakes are much higher. Mistakes could hurt the future of large groups of people.

The size of the membership and their families in the union I represented, District Council 37, could constitute the fourth largest city in New York State. This was an awesome responsibility, and I prepared for negotiations with New York City and others with this in mind.

This chapter describes how I applied the basic principles of negotiating in major, professional negotiations. It concludes with an analysis of the New York City fiscal crisis negotiations, the most complex negotiations of my career. There are lessons in these professional anecdotes for everyone interested in becoming a better negotiator.

WHOM DO YOU REPRESENT?

My union, District Council 37, has had some major negotiations with the city. Historically, DC 37 set the pattern for other unions. Because of this, we had to recognize the needs of the other unions since they were affected by our negotiations even though they were not directly involved. Foremost in my mind were the needs of the people whom I directly represented, but my responsibilities to the other unions that had yet to settle on a contract had to be taken into account as well. For example, although we set the pattern for the nonuniformed forces, I was always aware of the fact that the police and fire unions were watching intently. They always used our settlement as a benchmark, and then demanded a little more.

In major negotiations, this is not unusual and can be quite disturbing. You dislike being tied to the pattern setter; it diminishes your pride and power. Since they had the full support of Mayor Koch, the uniformed forces could escalate their terms with him after DC 37's settlement. They would always do slightly better than us, and I was upset by this. The membership of DC 37 couldn't care less, so my ego took second place. The members were more important. You don't negotiate for yourself, but for those whom you represent.

The heterogeneity of the membership of DC 37 was magnificent—backbreaking perhaps and beset with problems—but it was the diversity of the union that made it intriguing and exciting for me, especially during negotiations. A union of this size and diversity (the largest urban union in the country) required an enormous amount of outreach and preparation.

The two largest ethnic groups in our union were the African American membership and the Italian membership. Our union was so large that I believe we had the largest black and Italian membership of any other union in the city. In smaller numbers we had Hispanic, Jewish, and most other ethnic groups in our membership. In fact, in the accountants local, we had a large Egyptian group. They were bright, they were difficult, and they gave me a hard time, but in the most democratic fashion. It was a pleasure to argue with them.

Competing Needs and Double Negotiations

In major negotiations, there are often competing needs and goals among those you represent. This requires you to negotiate with your own people until they are unified prior to negotiating with your adversary. In order to do this, I had to understand the diversity of my union. In addition to the professional and ethnic diversity, we had the typical differences that exist in almost every union. We had older and younger groups. The younger people, focusing on the events of the moment, usually looked at wages and benefits. The older group would scrutinize retirement and security-related issues for the coming years. In order to fulfill its mission, the union couldn't just negotiate wages and benefits but had to be sensitive to the needs of the senior unionists—not only about their material retirement, but also their mental retirement: what they were going to do once they left their occupational activity.

In addition, I had to acknowledge the leaders of these individual groups. They were, in effect, my kitchen cabinet. I was fortunate in one sense that we had a decentralized union. I had many locals that were represented by jurisdictions, for example, the laborers locals; the professionals, engineers, and architects local; the hospital local. Each of these groups elected its own leadership. Although I was dealing with numerous groups, they were cohesive.

My professional staff would give me an analysis of the leadership of these locals. I would depend on my treasurer, Arthur Tibaldi, for fiscal information. My number-two person, Lillian Roberts, came out of the hospital system, where she had worked as a nurse's aide. Her insights about the rank and file were extremely helpful and essential to the first phase of the negotiations—those with the people I represented. Knowing the needs of those you represent is paramount.

Stakeholder Involvement and Participation

For any large organization—a union, corporation, public agency—direct involvement of the stakeholders is necessary to ensure that the negotiator understands the demands of those in the trenches and to build a framework of trust and support to see the negotiations through to completion. The best way to provide the negotiator with the facts he or she needs, and the stakeholders with the assurance that they are being appropriately represented, is through a formal process for their involvement.

Given the size and the complexity of the union, we set up a democratic mechanism that would filter out all of these differences and blend these needs into one major series of demands that we would present to the city.

The hierarchy for preparation was local union involvement, local leadership involvement, and finally committees to address major issues. The local unions had their own negotiations committee to present their members' demands. These demands would then come to the overall negotiations committees, composed of representatives from the locals. Most important was the Executive Committee, the chief policy body, with the greatest influence in shaping the demands, modifying them, making them realistic, discussing them, and packaging them in a document that was cohesive and reasonable. The key thing we did was recognize the need for, and provide a vehicle for, participation and involvement.

The participation and involvement of the membership during the preparation phase ensured that once the contract was negotiated, it would be ratified by the rank and file.

By contrast, the lack of involvement and participation of the players and their agents wounded the National Basketball Players Association (NBPA) in its 1995 negotiations. Simon Gourdine, who was general counsel for the NBPA, took over as executive director when the top man surprisingly resigned from the organization. Gourdine had an immediate baptism as chief negotiator. With little time to adjust, he found himself in an impossible situation.

The management executive, NBA commissioner David Stern, was almost deified by the club owners. He rose to power in the NBA because of the exceptional progress made by the basketball clubs. They grew to rival baseball, football, and hockey in terms of prestige and profit. David Stern received justifiable credit for the improvement in the fortunes of the NBA.

When Gourdine took over, he needed time and assistance. Regrettably, he did not reach out for assistance. To compound his misfortune, he was overpowered by Stern, who insisted on a contract in short order. Gourdine complied and in doing so, left some of the major players and their agents feeling they'd been shut out of the process. In fact, they claimed to have little or no understanding of the contents of the negotiated agreement.

It is of small consequence whether the players overreacted. The fact that some of the most powerful players insisted they were uninformed placed the chief negotiator, Gourdine, in an impossible situation. He was new, he was overshadowed by management's negotiator, and he was the target of criticism by an important part of his membership.

There were some understandable roadblocks for Gourdine in addition to his newness on the job. His constituency was spread out nationally. They were beholden to agents who helped make them very rich. Contact and communication were not easy—but they were a necessity. Gourdine acquiesced to Stern's timetable, and that left him little time for outreach. A more experienced person might have insisted on some more time to plan for the negotiations.

Gourdine compounded his problems by failing to enlist the expertise of others. The resources may have been available to him, but he never utilized them, and this very good man took a bad beating. Lacking the support of top players, Sy Gourdine did not last.

Not knowing about a good thing can be worse than knowing about a bad thing. People don't want to be left out of the process. The time and energy it takes to keep those you represent informed is a worthwhile necessity. Even more important is creating a mechanism for representation. It relieves the negotiator of the burden of being the sole decision-maker. It helps in obtaining the agreement of allies. I take pride in the fact that in hundreds of negotiated contracts, only one local ever refused to ratify an agreement I negotiated. I blamed this on management (an easy out for any union leader).

No Substitute for Knowledge

Negotiating is not a process that necessarily comes naturally. Experts in the field, good negotiators improve with practice. The more they negotiate, the better they get. But practice and process are useless unless they know the subject, the people involved, the pitfalls, and the facts. This fact-finding is absolutely critical to preparation.

Since the beginning of her tenure in 1994 as executive director for the New-York Historical Society, my wife, Betsy, has been involved in a series of major negotiations, all of which have one common goal: the economic solvency of the society. Decades of mismanagement and neglect had left this institution in financial ruin and its landmark building on Central Park West in terrible condition. The collection itself—artwork, artifacts—had been removed from the building for its own protection. The building was a symbol of the other troubles the society was facing. Although there was a plan to renovate the building, there was no plan to move the society forward and to consider its future (many thought it did not have a future) with a clear vision based in reality and fact.

Today, the society is thriving and stands poised for an expanded role. When I asked Betsy how she was able to negotiate her way through the minefields, her answer was brief and to the point: study the facts, get the information one way or another, prioritize the needs, and develop an ironclad plan to ensure winning each negotiation. The early successes are the building blocks for the negotiations to come. With winning come trust and confidence, two qualitites that had long been eroded at the society.

Betsy's first priority was the building. The roof leaked, water was infiltrating the walls of the library stacks, the top floor was completely shut down, and the collections that were intended to be housed on the fourth floor, now closed, were in leased storage space at a hefty cost, straining an already meager annual operating budget. The good news was that there existed a long-dormant construction project with adequate funding to make the building watertight and to redesign and modernize the first-floor facilities to bring them to more functional standards.

Prior to Betsy's arrival, the construction company was happily collecting a monthly retainer, while the project lay dormant. During Betsy's initial negotiations with the construction company, she was faced with demands for significant increases over the original estimates. Betsy knew she needed facts. What were the original scope and cost estimate of the project? Why had the costs increased? What did the construction company's contract require in terms of cost overruns?

Since construction was not Betsy's background, she called on experts to evaluate the little documentation that was available. The experts' findings were that the scope of the project had changed. The construction contract clearly indicated that no change in the plan could be made without the written approval of the executive director or her designee. Instead, the construction company's people had held meetings with many of the individual departments at the society and had changed the plans according to the whims of those department heads. This is planning in a vacuum. There was no overall direction.

When Betsy brought in her technical ammunition, the negotiations were brief and to the point. "Where are the signed approvals for these changes?" she asked. "Why has the cost for the electrical upgrade increased tenfold? What were your original estimates based on?"

In addition to supporting her case with the facts, Betsy, realizing that the real decision-makers were at the construction company's headquarters, let it be known through a major New York developer friend that she meant business. She would not be a pushover in these negotiations. If the situation didn't change, the company would take a bigger beating in the long run in terms of time and money.

So back at the negotiating table, with the construction company's representatives, Betsy appointed her CFO and an architect friend to manage the project closely from that day forward. The society was scheduled to reopen in May, and it was now December. Work had still not begun. The negotiations ended with the construction estimates back within the budget and with an aggressive plan to move the project to its completion by May. The project was completed two days before the opening gala.

This first and important success marked the beginning of a change in attitude in both the staff of the society and its trustees. In the past, negotiations with the trustees had been fruitless in terms of their financial contributions. Betsy's clear vision, coupled with her early success on the building project, led to the next step in the society's rejuvenation: the creation of what would be called the Luce Center.

Now that the building would be watertight, a plan for returning the collection from expensive storage space was feasible. As a result, the Henry Luce Foundation contributed $7.5 million to design and construct the fourth-floor study and storage center, and to catalog the collection in a database. With this project underway and the trust and the confidence of the trustees restored, Betsy moved on the final piece of her plan: to modernize and integrate the society's famous library with the society's collection.

The Mellon Foundation seemed interested in assisting the society, but their experience with previous society administrators had left them cautious, even resistant. Betsy's solid plan and the renewed confidence in the ability of the society to move forward were augmented by the prestige and position of one board member, Colin Campbell. Colin enlisted the board's support for Betsy's plan to affiliate with New York University. The deal that was ultimately consummated with NYU could not have happened with previous society administrations and the previously fractured board. Now, as one success has built on the next, trust has replaced mistrust. It all started with knowledge and fact finding.

There is just no substitute for knowledge. You must recognize that negotiating is not just a process; you must know the facts, and you must know yourself. All of us may negotiate at one time or another, but some people should leave it to others. Betsy relied on her CFO and an architect (working under her supervision) to negotiate the day-to-day details of the society's construction project. The person you designate could be a member of the family, a lawyer, a friend who understands and knows negotiations.

I am a lousy numbers person. I always knew where the numbers were going and I always had a good general idea of the outcome, but I needed to know more than that. I needed to know specific numbers and percentages. Even a few pennies could hurt the people I represented. I was very fortunate in that I always had someone whom I would call a numbers person at my side in major negotiations. He kept me from making mistakes—sometimes bad mistakes.

In negotiations, if you have the facts and your opposition doesn't, they will be on the defensive. It is an easy triumph when you can come up with a number or a piece of information that leaves your adversary mumbling.

Knowing how and when to use information is as important as having it. You also need to know when to hold back. Spouting too many facts can give you an air of arrogance and make you sound demeaning. You can never know too much, but don't use it to excess. There are enough smart alecks in the world.

Your knowledge of power is also vitally important. What is the strength of your adversary? What is your strength? Whom does the mayor listen to? Whom does the landlord listen to? Your boss? Your customer or supplier? What are their prevailing interests in the negotiations? You cannot overlook this. You have to measure your ability and your power in relation to the people on the other side of the table. If you don't have power on your side, if you can't move your adversary, then advance your principles. As British prime minister Tony Blair has said, "Power without principle is barren."

Comparing Settlements

In preparing for any negotiation, your knowledge base includes studying and understanding recent comparable settlements, if available. Patterns are set by negotiations. Somebody buys a home in a neighborhood where many homes are up for sale, and this particular sale is a barometer for the neighborhood. Both sellers and buyers take a very close look at it. In labor relations, a major union will make a settlement where management has acquiesced. Both labor and management in other areas then consider the outcome of that settlement in their negotiations. This doesn't mean the results will be exactly the same, but those who negotiate after a major settlement are weakened or strengthened by that settlement. In New York City, firefighters will study settlements made by the police, teachers, and other city unions. The union that settles first with the city becomes the barometer.

Comparisons, however, are grounded by the period in which they occur, mainly because the environmental factors are of that moment. If there is inflation for one period of time, it will affect all negotiations—labor, home sales, almost any kind of consumer activity that calls for negotiations. A negotiation that was beneficial to you two or three years ago will have little meaning in current negotiations. Your comparisons should be relevent in the context of the current market.

Using Precedents

As with recent comparative settlements, your knowledge of past precedents and practices will be instrumental in helping you define the context of the talks. For any negotiations, particularly those involving contractual agreements, past practices and precedents are considered nonnegotiable by those they favor. Those they do not favor recognize the power of a precedent and often find such precedents difficult to alter. It is rare when a previously won issue is given up in subsequent contract negotiations. Precedents can be changed, as can contractual obligations. However, what has come into existence in the past cannot be unilaterally taken away. It should be done by an agreement involving both parties.

The precedent of summer hours for New York City employees is an excellent example of tradition that had become meaningless. Prior to air-conditioning of municipal offices and workplaces, Mayor Robert Wagner instituted a program of summer hours. From June to the end of September, workers with a thirty-five-hour week were permitted to leave an hour earlier every day, resulting in a thirty-hour week. As offices were later air-conditioned, the thirty-hour week remained.

John Lindsay, Mayor Wagner's successor, was furious with this outmoded practice and unilaterally issued an executive order that did away with summer hours. Union membership went berserk. Hell hath no fury like a worker arbitrarily deprived of a benefit. The union protested, and Lindsay wanted to know how "in God's name" I could justify this. I couldn't. But I also could not allow him to make changes unilaterally.

Because of precedent, my position was that both sides had to agree to change. Lindsay insisted we take it to arbitration. The arbitrator said that Lindsay was wrong. In one of the mayor's rare vulgar moments, he angrily assured me that he'd bring it to the collective bargaining table. I answered, "We will work it out." I'll tell you how we did that.

PREPARING TO LOSE

As a person, you can be gracious and graceful. As a negotiator, representing other people, you have to consider their feelings. On the summer hours issue, I had some private meetings with Herb Haber, Lindsay's newly appointed negotiator. I told Herb that I could diminish summer hours, but not all at once. And the union should receive something in return.

We worked it out so that at the end of negotiations, when exhaustion was setting in, he'd give me a welfare improvement. In turn, I would cut back the months for summer hours. He was delighted, and it worked. Some of my top rank-and-file leaders had agreed to this "giveback" beforehand.

This agreement served two purposes. The summer hours issue would have put the union on the defensive and would have adulterated our other demands. Since management had been apprised of and had agreed to the plan, the importance of that issue was diminished. In addition, I thought the summer hours issue was damned embarrassing. Not only was it difficult to defend, but the forty-hour workers, who did not share in summer hours, were upset by the benefit.

If you prepare to concede on an issue, you can ameliorate the effects. Where you have a loser, you level with your membership. My newness did not give me the security to involve the membership on the summer hours issue. However, I did confer with some of the major local union presidents. If the experience had occurred later in my tenure, I'd have made it an open issue with the membership. This was a reflection of my power and authority at that point.

My policy is never to mislead the membership. If you do, it comes back to haunt you. When you prepare yourself to lose on an issue, you should also prepare the members. In 1975 during the fiscal crisis, I had opportunities to do that—too many opportunities.

THE FISCAL CRISIS

In the fall of 1974, New York City found itself in an unprecedented critical situation. The city did not have the money to pay the interest due on outstanding municipal bonds. On the brink of economic default, the city was at the edge of disaster. The enormity of the crisis and its implications for radical change in the life and status of the city, its people, even the nation as a whole, made for an incredible challenge to labor, management, government, and corporate institutions. The whole world seemed to be standing on its head, yet somehow the city would have to come out of it. We had to find a solution.

The ensuing negotiations that led to a solution were the most intricate and complex of my career. It's hard to imagine a negotiating situation with higher stakes and fewer options other than one that involves the possibility of war. In addition to losing its fiscal autonomy, New York City was faced with the potential loss of fifty thousand jobs and major service upheavals, such as the takeover of the City University system by the state, the privatization of municipal hospitals, and social service cuts, including welfare.

Despite the magnitude of the negotiations, the basic principles of negotiating applied and resulted in a solution to the crisis—as well as a stronger, more cohesive union.

Looking at Yourself as a Negotiator

For the first time in my career, I was going into negotiations with the upsetting purpose of giving up money and benefits the union had previously negotiated. My entire career was dedicated to raising the standard of living of the people I represented, yet I knew the union had no alternative. The union and its members had roots in the community. Most of them didn't have suburban mobility. A solvent and independent New York City was an imperative for those I represented. There wasn't any question of sacrificing for New York City; our membership *was* New York City. Any suffering the city endured, our membership endured. We had to identify with the city.

To complicate matters, there were no legal or practical solutions to study or to use as models since no other major city had ever reached the threshold of default at that time. Worse, time was not on the union's side. The city was in a rapid downward spiral, reeling with anxiety. We had to move quickly.

The most overwhelming difficulty was that five levels of negotiations would be required. The state and federal governments, the bankers, the city, and the municipal unions each had a stake and a role to play in the negotiations. The various unions would need to synchronize, coordinate, and reach agreement with disparate constituencies.

The unions were represented by me, Barry Feinstein of the Teamsters, and, to a lesser extent, John DeLury of the sanitation workers. DeLury relied totally on Jack Bigel, the unions' main professional support. Another powerful union, the United Federation of Teachers, was in a weakened position. Union president Al Shanker tried to carry water on both shoulders. He was running the national union and the American Federation of Teachers, and working out of Washington, D.C. It was almost impossible for him to do justice to the New York City teachers without being in the city full time. Unfortunately, he failed to delegate authority to two talented people who could have done the job: his protégé and number-two person, Sandra Feldman, and the late Bill Scott.

The union leadership representing police and firefighters could not control their membership. They refused to participate in the negotiations and be a party to any givebacks. So, it was me, Barry Feinstein, McFeeley, Vizzini, and Jack Bigel on the unions' side of the table.

Looking at Your Adversary

Unlike previous negotiations between the city and the unions, these talks required us to reach agreement with a player who came to the table but had no intention of negotiating: the bankers. This was unique and almost beyond comprehension. Felix Rohatyn, the governor's representative, also represented the corporate interests in the talks. Bill Ellinghaus of AT&T wisely deferred his role as corporate negotiator to Felix. Felix's charge from Governor Carey was to get a settlement with a minimum of pain. Felix accepted the challenge. His prestigious background as a major investment banker calmed the nerves of the corporate and banking world. In the end, it was Felix's skills as a mediator, not a negotiator, that would lead the city out of the crisis. As a mediator, he facitilated the process of the negotiations.

If the city and the unions had an Achilles heel, it was the federal government, which did not like New York. In fact, Washington was antagonistic toward New York City. In order to obtain the feds' assistance, we would have to overcome their negative prejudices and misinformation. The assistance we were seeking consisted of federal loans and guarantees. The borrowing we sought would be paid back with interest, a fact few people mentioned. (And eventually it was all repaid.)

The Stakes in the Negotiations

New York City was $13 billion in the hole—the equivalent of 25 percent of all local debt in the United States. The apparent stake was default itself, a concept we could not fully comprehend. We did understand one thing: default meant the courts would decide what to do, and New York City would be at the mercy of the judiciary.

The possible loss of fifty thousand jobs coupled with severe service cuts were perhaps the more tangible consequences of default. The city's loss of autonomy and prestige, while less tangible, were equally troubling, especially since we could only guess at what that would mean.

Labor agreed on a bottom line. If sacrifices were to be made, we insisted on these guidelines:

- The sacrifice would be proportional to the ability to give.
- Lower economic workers would sacrifice less than higher-paid workers.
- The diminishment of the workforce would first occur through attrition, then through firing provisional workers, with permanent civil servant cuts a last resort.
- The collective bargaining process would remain intact.
- The negotiations would require agreement from both sides.

The city and the state, through Mayor Beame's representative Jim Cavanaugh and Felix Rohatyn, needed a settlement that would be acceptable to both Washington and Albany. Without the support of these two entities, default would be a foregone conclusion. The state controlled the negotiations and played the mayor hard. Felix's relationship with Warren Anderson, the leader of the Republican-dominated state senate, was positive. We were all grateful for Anderson's leadership. He didn't carry the upstate anticity prejudices of many of his colleagues.

The negotiations between the unions and the city and state were cordial, but the governments wanted more sacrifice from the workforce. They did not want to err on the side of leniency. Nevertheless, we found a constructive road to agreement. There were no ultimatums, and we kept talking.

The city and the state put their major demand on the table: a 6 percent decrease in wages. The unions' counteroffer was a three-tier wage loan, which would ultimately be returned to the workers:

- Workers earning less than $10,000 would lend 2 percent.
- Workers earning $10,000 to $15,000 would lend 4 percent.
- Workers earning more than $15,000 would lend 6 percent.

But a unified approach was lacking because Al Shanker refused to go along. In general the teachers were earning above $15,000. I was now doing double negotiations. I explained to Al that the money was a loan that would be repaid. I also explained that many of the professionals represented by DC 37 earned more than $15,000. I stressed the fairness of the sliding scale to city workers as a whole.

Al was not buying. He wanted out of the negotiating coalition but wanted to remain as an observer. In no uncertain terms I told him he was either in or out. Al was obdurate, but I said that I wasn't about to tolerate someone who wouldn't put himself on the line with me. Al left. We had lost an important constituent, and the teachers lost any voice in the outcome. As a result, they eventually paid a higher price than any other union.

Back at the bargaining table, Felix was ready to accept the loan formula, but he exacted strict terms for repayment. The state and federal loans were predicated on a balanced city budget for three straight years. It was a significant victory for him when we accepted this. The unions would now be held accountable for balancing the budget.

The Context of the Talks

With the union agreement in hand, the talks now expanded to include the bankers and corporate negotiators. The city needed $2.5 billion in new money to stay solvent, but the banks would not lend any new funds. The best they would do was to extend the term of existing debt, giving the city additional time to pay. The city then asked the unions for a $2 billion loan from pension funds. They were asking to take the retirees' capital to stabilize the lives of the members who were still working. I recognized that I needed outside help and sought the advice of the international union, the AFL-CIO, as well as Jack Bigel.

The consensus was that the risk was worth taking. In fact, we had little alternative. The city needed the money, and the corporate world would give zilch. The unions' contribution would stabilize the situation and make for more secure pensions in future years.

When we agreed to the request, the senior workers, who were the ones with the most to lose since they were on the verge of retirement, were magnificent. Senior union members have a great deal of power. A protest from them would have weakened my stance at the bargaining table. They accepted the agreement we negotiated. The overwhelming fact, which they understood, was that the pension reserve was the only possible source of new money.

The unions in turn exacted some gains from the city and state. The state agreed to provide the city with $2.3 billion in order to keep it solvent through 1975. Most important, the negotiations led to a united front in Washington. The city received a federal loan guarantee, and mutually agreed-on new taxes were passed. The banks and bondholders agreed to refinance existing loans and declared a moratorium on certain critical payments.

While the city, state, and federal governments made important contributions, the corporations gave very little indeed. There were exceptions, such as Lew Rudin and other major real estate owners, who agreed to prepay property taxes—the Rudin brothers were a magnificent bridge between the unions and the governmental hierarchy—but in the main it was the unions that contributed the most.

Although the unions gave a great deal in the negotiations, we also had the most to lose. This fact, and our understanding of the context of the talks, put the unions in a weakened position. All's well that ends well. Although there were layoffs during the crisis and soon after, as the economy grew, the new Koch administration restored the lost jobs by expanding the workforce. We had given up a great deal, but we managed to minimize the sacrifice to the working lives of our members. We in the unions had observed the basic principles of negotiating, and the outcome was as much as we could have hoped for.

Chapter Six

WOMEN AND NEGOTIATIONS

Women have failed to break through the gender barrier in the area of negotiations. Changes in their traditional roles as housewife and mother have made working women the norm in our society, yet despite the dramatic increase in their numbers in the workforce, women are still rarely seen at the bargaining table. Where women have been invited in, they have either been tokens or representatives in professions traditionally associated with women. A small part of the failure is due to women's own resistance to negotiating, but the major barrier has been sexism. If men wanted women to participate as equal partners, there would be no women's movement, or this chapter, or any need on the part of women to organize and fight for their rights. But men will not move over.

The fight for equality is just that—a fight. People do not easily give up power or prestige. You have to insist on your deserved share and take it away. As Mary Pickford said, "Failure is not falling down, it's staying down." Women will have to stand up and take down the barriers without the help of men, or they will continue to be underpaid and trapped under a glass ceiling.

The first step is for women to understand their own attitude toward negotiating and recognize that it is inseparable from their perception of their rights as women in general. The second step is for women to demand involvement in negotiations in order to gain the experience and security they need.

The importance of power in negotiations has already been covered, and women, who have traditionally been denied power, may feel uncomfortable at the bargaining table. Being submissive and accommodating—as women have been taught to be—are characteristics that are undesirable in the environment of negotiations. On the other hand, there are those who contend that women can see both sides of an argument more clearly and willingly than men, and that women can identify with adversaries much better than men. These qualities can be useful to negotiators.

The initial demand of the women's movement for equal rights, and the enabling legislation that followed, were the easy parts. As with most other revolutions, however, the required changes in attitudes are much more difficult and take longer to achieve.

NEGOTIATING BEGINS AT HOME

Women's roles have changed, and in many areas women have attained equal footing with men. But particularly in the more personal aspects of life, love, and family, it is still a male society. Even the most gifted women somehow find themselves catering to men in a man's world. My three daughters-in-law are examples of this syndrome.

Betsy and I are very lucky. We love my children and her child, and we've had tremendous satisfaction in their spousal choices. Our daughters-in-law are three of the nicest and most talented professional women, yet each put her own career on hold for the sake of her husband's career.

My sons are not lightweights. Each is gifted and successful in his own way. However, in this world of women's liberation, of women's freedom, of women's fight to get to the top, not one of my wonderful, talented daughters-in-law has insisted on being first, taking the lead, calling the shots. They take for granted that the man has the ultimate responsibility to bring home the pork chops.

It brings to mind what Gloria Steinem stated at an international union conference: "The fight begins in the minds of all of us. It begins everywhere and every place with every woman." The shifting of the decision of who's on first is both necessary and possible. I have experienced it firsthand in my own marriage and appreciate the resulting mutual individual growth and strengthening of our relationship. Betsy and I are most fortunate.

Like most of her contemporaries, Betsy was raised in a man's world. Women didn't confront or negotiate. In her home, women didn't even disagree or argue. Education meant preparation for marriage and family rather than for a productive career. The husband was considered the dominant figure, the wife almost an appendage to him. Divorce wasn't an option, especially if it was the woman who wanted out.

Given her background and upbringing, when Betsy's first marriage became unacceptable to her, she was not only frightened by the notion of the divorce proceedings to come, but became completely dependent on others. However well intentioned, her brother-in-law took over and selected an attorney to represent her. Betsy never questioned his choice and never questioned the attorney's advice.

She was on the defensive from the beginning. Since she was the spouse who was calling it quits, she was considered the cause of the divorce. Her own attorney insisted that she must bear the burden of being the one who wanted to leave. She was the villain, her husband the victim. Her attorney not only made her feel guilty; he led her to believe she could lose custody of their child. There were no negotiations, and the case was settled very much in her husband's favor. He received most of the assets of the marriage, and she received a meager child support agreement. Betsy questioned none of this. Fortunately, times change.

During the first fourteen years of our relationship, Betsy assumed the traditional, secondary role. I was in a position of prestige and had a certain degree of power. Not only was I the head of the major union in New York City, I was the first American to head the Public Service International, a trade union secretariat attached to the International Labor Organization. This position required a great deal of traveling, and coupled with my responsibilities in New York, my agenda was full.

Betsy accompanied me on many trips, and I was grateful for her knowledge of four languages. She was comfortable among the international trade unionists and did a great deal of translating for me. In the international trade union field there are translators in formal sessions, but at social gatherings and informal sessions life could be very difficult for a monolinguist like myself. Betsy was incredibly helpful.

Back in New York, Betsy continued to play the secondary role. Although she was sought after for work in the public sector, she was hesitant to accept. So while Betsy took some important jobs in venture capitalism and in heading up foundations, her primary concern was to make certain that I was comfortable.

At the age of sixty-five, I retired, believing that too many trade unionists hang around much too long and don't allow for change at the top. Betsy blossomed. She became a major player in the mayoral campaign of David Dinkins. She held the key treasury role and was the major fund raiser. She made certain the candidate met important people with deep pockets. She was indefatigable. It is no secret that an African American political candidate finds it terribly difficult to raise funds. Betsy took care of this, with great success. After Dinkins's victory, she was rewarded with the job of parks commissioner.

She was a first-rate, hands-on administrator who not only managed the day-to-day operations but initiated and developed a voluntary organization for fund raising. The Parks Foundation subsequently raised millions of dollars for city parks at a time when public funding was dwindling. As I have mentioned, she is now working as the executive director of the New-York Historical Society, again with great success.

What if I hadn't retired? A difficult question to answer.

In these later years of our relationship, it's Betsy who's on first, as it should be. That is important to me. The fact that this was fortuitous is of small consequence. Our roles changed, and the change has made for a richer relationship between us. As Besty grows in ability, prestige, and importance, I love it.

As Betsy became more secure, she also became less afraid to argue. She became less afraid to disagree. She argues her points strongly and does not back down. While she still dislikes "doing the bargaining," as she puts it, this is of small importance.

Most important, Betsy acknowledges her own growth in her ability to assert herself. Often she would declare, "I wouldn't have done this years ago." And she wouldn't have. In a way, it's a sad testimony to the number of women with strong ability and potential who are held back from making a full contribution.

OVERCOMING GENDER-BASED OBSTACLES

One of the biggest obstacles women face is their own prejudicial belief that men are better equipped to deal with the rough-and-tumble nature of negotiations. Centuries of repression have left scars that cannot be healed in the thirty years since the women's movement took shape. Today's thirty-something working woman typically was raised in a nuclear family with traditional gender-based roles. Her lifestyle may be very different from her mother's, but she may still harbor the values and beliefs she was taught as a child.

During a luncheon at my house, the woman seated next to me asked me quite bluntly and simply, "How do you negotiate?" I asked for some background. What did she mean? It seems she was part of a small group that represented an international company here in the United States. The group had done extremely well in a matter of a few years and had tripled the profits of the company, helping it to become profitable. Yet her increase in salary for this achievement was very small indeed. She was frustrated and extremely upset by this and asked me what she could do about it. I told her, "You just do it."

I pointed out to her that she needed to decide what she wanted. If you represent yourself, you have to define what your needs are. It was strange, but she had never thought of this. It was as though this was the first time it occurred to her that her needs should drive the talks. Her frustration was very deep. I asked her to give me an idea of what she believed her compensation should be. She mentioned the desired wage increase. She mentioned some security factors. All of these were reasonable in view of her importance to the firm and her skills and I told her so. I advised her that she had to put these demands forward. She reacted with frustration, to the point of seeming frightened by the whole activity.

I told her that if she couldn't do it, she should get someone to do it for her. She couldn't continue to allow herself to be exploited. She appeared to be tortured by the whole conversation and probably regretted ever having asked for my advice.

Logically, this highly talented professional woman who obviously produced for her firm should have been secure about the situation. Yet she was afraid to ask for her deserved reward. She just couldn't seem to do it, and it was terribly sad. She was suffering the pain of being in a man's world, where women were told they don't ask and they don't negotiate.

Betsy and I discussed it. Betsy's analysis was quite interesting. She described the culture in which she was raised. Women were told that it was not ladylike to negotiate just as it was not ladylike to "quarrel" and make a point. The inherent confrontational aspect of negotiating compounds the difficulty that women of this culture have in negotiating.

Barbara Isenberg is the founder and creative director of a successful international company that markets toy bears. Despite her talent and success, she derides her ability as a negotiator. In her own words, "I don't enjoy confrontation. I prefer to have other people within the organization perform the negotiations. My brother and other *men* in the organization do the negotiating."

Barbara recently had an experience that changed her attitude.

Shortly before Christmas, her company received a shipment of toy bears manufactured in Korea. She took one look at a sample and exclaimed, "These are dog-faced bears. They're unacceptable and must be replaced!" The bears were not only poorly designed; the quality of the materials and the workmanship were inferior.

The men in the company insisted that she "had no choice." Christmas was drawing near, and she had no time to replace the shipment with a new one. The more aggressive and insistent they became, the more Barbara resolved to rectify the situation. She was not willing to market an inferior product. She realized that her male colleagues would not be able to make her case with the Korean factory owners, since they felt she was being frivolous. They did not have the same sensitivity to quality and design that she did. So much for Barbara's claim to be nonconfrontational. She went for broke.

She contacted the Korean factory owners and told them they had made a mistake and would have to correct it immediately. Her adversaries initially balked and tried instead to negotiate a lower price for the bears, but Barbara would not budge. She stood her ground and won. For Barbara, a shipment of dog-faced bears inspired her to overcome her gender-based obstacles to negotiating.

Alexandra Penney, a gifted editor and writer and a close friend, has no difficulty negotiating with writers and other professionals. She also has the Betsy Gotbaum characteristic: outside of her professional capacity, she hates to engage in negotiations. She asked for my help in the rental of a summer home in Quogue on Long Island.

Alexandra and her boyfriend had zeroed in on a house to rent. It was the only place they really liked. There was another bid on the house so time was not on her side. The rental would not remain on the market.

On the positive side, the landlord liked the fact that they were a young couple without children or pets. She had had previous tenants who had damaged the house and furnishings. This was a major plus for Alexandra and her boyfriend.

The landlord was asking $35,000 for July and August. While

Alexandra originally wanted to rent for five months, from May through September, she made a counteroffer of $30,000 for four months. There was now a disparity of two months and $5,000.

I asked Alexandra for her bottom line. Although the numbers were not written in stone, at least it would give her discipline. It would fix in her mind where she wanted to finish. She replied $30,000 and three to four months.

I recommended she make a counteroffer of $28,000 for two months and two weeks. This would give her the room in the negotiations to increase the dollars and extend the time. It worked. The landlord really wanted Alexandra and her boyfriend as tenants. They settled on $30,000 for three months.

It is always of concern when women who are involved in complex professional negotiations find personal and everyday negotiations difficult. There is a way in which women can overcome their dislike for or discomfort with negotiations. If you don't like negotiations, if you feel you can't do it, you shouldn't be the main negotiator. But women should not completely avoid negotiations. They would be far better advised to sit in on negotiations or to make any other kind of contribution they want. They need the exposure and the experience. People grow into it.

After nine years and two children, a friend of mine wanted out of her marriage to a very controlling husband. Communication had ceased, and her husband's idea of negotiating was to say, "It's my way or no way."

At the beginning of their marriage, she had left her job and was not prepared now to support herself financially. She also wanted the divorce settled peacefully out of court. She acknowledged this as a "woman's thing." Her husband tried to take advantage of the situation. Whatever he offered, he treated as largess. He negotiated with her from both sides of the table and completely overwhelmed her.

Therapy came in the person of a woman lawyer who helped her evaluate the situation. "Forget about his demands. What do you need?" After they had prepared a detailed projection of her expenses and contingency needs, her lawyer asked whether my friend could do any of the negotiating. My friend was certain that she did not know how to negotiate; indeed, the very thought of it made her nervous. Her lawyer explained that as her legal representative, there was nothing unusual or wrong with her handling the bargaining for her client. However, this sensitive lawyer felt that my friend's participation in the negotiations could strengthen her shaky self-esteem and lack of confidence, so she insisted that my friend be at the table.

It worked out beautifully. Although my friend did almost no negotiating, she comfortably engaged in the process, advising her lawyer of her husband's errors of omission and commission as necessary. The negotiations resulted in a settlement close to her bottom line. More important, the experience itself taught her to be more objective and assertive about her own needs. It gave her confidence about her ability to negotiate.

She has since met and married an accomplished and understanding man. When she discusses her first marriage, she says, "I wish I had the strength I have now. He could never get away with his demands today." My friend has the satisfaction of realizing her own growth.

The easiest way to overcome gender-based obstacles is by acknowledging them in the first place. As with most other bias, once you look at it objectively, you see that it is irrational.

A close friend, an executive working in a public sector job in the male-dominated field of design and construction, has been quite successful in negotiating with architects, contractors, construction managers, and real estate professionals. Since most of the negotiations she's involved in pit her against male adversaries with their usual prejudices toward women, she has developed a strategy for certain situations in which she uses the adversary's bias to her own advantage.

Realizing the contractor sitting across the table probably thinks that she's inadequate, she opens the talks by asking seemingly simple-minded questions about the project. The contractor, from what he views as his superior position, proceeds to discuss his construction plans, costs, materials, and labor needs, during which time she takes copious notes. When his monologue is complete, she zeros in with more pointed, specific questions. Since the contractor has already admitted to certain procedures and their associated cost estimates, she goes in for the kill by recommending optional, more cost-effective strategies. My friend then serves up a generous helping of principle for the finish by stressing the importance of the project to the end users and to the city as a whole, the importance of doing more with less in tough fiscal times, and her commitment to being a good client to the contractor by making timely payments and decisions.

The interesting thing is that this woman is able to negotiate so effectively only because the issue at stake is not personal, but rather involves her professional crusade. She has knowledge on her side and is strongly motivated and empowered by the importance of the outcome to her clients. In addition, men underestimate her. This gives her an advantage that she exploits, which is difficult for her adversaries to overcome.

WOMEN AND WAGES

The single most important indicator of women's status in society is their compensation relative to that of men. Levels of compensation do more than determine lifestyle. In our materialistic society, salary is also a strong indicator of prestige and position. Wages are the chief indicator of what your employer thinks you deserve. It is in this area that women really get short shrift.

When we compare women's wages to men's, we often remark on how women are pigeonholed into traditional women's jobs thanks to discrimination and unfair negotiations. These are the usual issues raised in the fight for gender equity.

An article in the July 17, 1994, issue of the Cleveland *Plain Dealer* notes that a male executive said that the problem with women is that they do not negotiate. He went on to say that the employer is not responsible for negotiating the salary on behalf of a candidate, male or female. He came up with the punch line, "Women with experience never ask for more than is offered." He added that, "Men usually do negotiate for more."

The statement implies that women are inferior as negotiators. It doesn't address the fact that most business environments prevent women from negotiating. Apparently this executive never asked himself why "men usually do negotiate for more." The sexism escaped him, but the unfortunate women working in his organization are victimized by it.

There have been some unconscionable disparities in salary levels between men and women. This is now beginning to change as women challenge these disparities.

In 1965, the beginning of my tenure as executive director of District Council 37, I was confronted with a blatant case of sex discrimination. Male cleaners of public buildings received more than women cleaners. This was rationalized by labeling the males as heavy-duty cleaners. The union examined the jobs. It was pure nonsense. Any heavy-duty work the men could perform, the women could do just as well. It was a crude and indefensible rationalization to keep their wages lower than the men. In a negotiations with the city, we wiped out the disparity.

There was also a blatant racial discrimination in this area. In the custodian position, which was a supervisory and higher-paid position than the cleaners, most of the incumbents were white males. The vast majority of the cleaners were black women. This was rectified by eliminating the cleaner title and replacing it with the titles Custodial I and Custodial Supervisor. All those in Custodial I would have promotional opportunities to the supervising position. The situation changed dramatically when the union succeeded in negotiating the change in titles. A quarter-century later, I found the very same blatant discrimination at the Board of Education, where the vast majority of higher-paid custodians, firemen (i.e., those who start up the boilers), and handymen are male, and the low-paid cleaners are women. This inequity is in large part due to the custodians themselves, who employ lower-echelon workers.

Inconsistencies between salaries of men and women exist at all job levels. For lower- or middle-income earners, such disparities are more troublesome and more difficult to resolve. A great deal of publicity is given to revolutions at the top, revolutions that should be publicized and do have meaning for women in negotiations. But working-class women are also discriminated against and receive little publicity.

Speaking of revolutions at the top, a few women in the tennis world, led by Billie Jean King, Chris Evert, and Martina Navratilova, fought for and won the fight for equal compensation with men. Previously the prizes for men had exceeded those for women in the same tournaments. The checks are now the same, and not surprisingly greater prestige and dignity for women's tennis have followed. The women became tough negotiators and they won, although from now on they cannot ever again afford to sit back. The regression in prize parity in the 1996 Australian Open should be a warning that the battle may be over, but the war is not yet won.

CHANGING MALE ATTITUDES

In negotiations, women who have managed to break through have a responsibility to help those who are struggling. They can encourage women to participate in negotiations and can give novices exposure to the negotiations process. But men have a responsibility too.

My own education and insight grew thanks to the dynamic change generated by the women's revolution. In the twenty years I have lived with Betsy, she has taught me a great deal as she grew in stature and security. Betsy helped me at home. Others helped me on the job.

Some years ago I was seeking a replacement for my general counsel. The number-two person was a woman who was an excellent lawyer but not a good administrator.

Beverly Gross, a lawyer with an excellent background, came for the job interview. Her credentials were good, but I had a major misgiving. If I hired another woman, the number-two person would quit. Beverly was impressive. Her negotiating skills were inspiring. She confronted me with a very simple question. "Would I raise the same objection if two men were involved?" I replied, "No, but . . ." and never finished my answer. Beverly was hired.

At a negotiations meeting, the city insisted that a budget deficit existed. We knew the numbers and argued the point. The city budget director, Alair Townsend, was not present. Instead, a male colleague was representing the city on the other side of the table. "Why don't you guys bring the lovely broad here and let her present the numbers. Besides, I'm tired of looking at you ugly bastards," I said with vulgar humor. The men didn't protest, but Beverly did. She took me aside and informed me that my actions and words were uncalled for and unacceptable. I protested that I meant no harm. In a very matter-of-fact tone, she insisted that I created harm. "What was it, Bev?" Bev's reply was short and to the point: "You insulted every woman sitting at the table."

I conceded that she was right and told her, "I'll be more careful in the future. I had no right to let my humor get out of hand." Beverly was insistent and tough and would never allow me any license.

The Betsys and Beverlys of this world go a long way in changing attitudes. The Victor Gotbaum of twenty years ago has changed for the better. Betsy refused to accept me as a done deed. When the question of sexism comes up, Betsy says, "He's doing fine, but he's still learning." I am fortunate to have good teachers.

Sexual harassment suits, on and off the job, may be the ultimate weapon in changing male attitudes. Similarly, bad publicity can make for change. Valerie Salembier, publisher of *Esquire* magazine, wrote about her experience while working at the *New York Post* in *Working Women* magazine. When there were complaints at the *Post* about Salembier's work, she asked for a formal review.

According to Salembier, during the review meeting, the men remained mute. They refused to comment and would not respond to her specific questions. Finally, she says, one said, "You are a nice girl, but we have to let you go."

Salembier agreed to leave with the understanding that they would be contractually required for pay her the remaining balance of her annual salary. They refused, offering her roughly half that amount. When she threatened to sue, they treated those threats with contempt.

Throughout the litigation, she claims, management continued to refer to her as a "nice girl." They had an array of lawyers lined up. She persisted. Not only did they have an inadequate case, they had a tiger by the tail—a female tiger. They settled, and she received her full compensation. Some people have to learn the hard way. Salembier's willingness to fight taught them a valuable lesson and made her a winner in this negotiation.

Chapter Seven

THREE'S A CROWD

There may come a time during negotiations (and it is usually quite obvious to both sides) when you have to face the fact that a negotiated settlement cannot be reached. The negotiators are not performing well, your remaining negotiating options will either put you in court or in the headlines, or the animosity between the adversaries has reached the boiling point and constructive talks are impossible. Whether it's a mother's intervention in a dispute between her children, a colleague's participation in a disagreement between coworkers, or a decision by labor leaders and management to retain the services of a mediator or arbitrator, the call is for outside help. No matter how you slice it, third-party intervention, as it is known, is an admission by both sides they can't resolve the negotiations on their own.

Third-party intervention (TPI), also called alternate dispute resolution, comes in two basic models: mediation and arbitration. There are other forms, such as fact finding and a mixture of mediation and arbitration called med-arb, but they are rarely used.

Mediation and arbitration are formal, professional labels for procedures that are regularly employed. Even the simplest negotiation between two parties may require outside intervention, and the same principles apply:

- TPI is not a substitute for negotiations and should be considered only in an impasse.
- The decision to bring in outside help cannot be made unilaterally. Both sides must be ready to open up the talks to others.
- There must be agreement on the mediator or arbitrator, or in everyday disputes, the adviser, friend, relative, or professional.

TPI is a tool of last resort. In general, I don't recommend it since it is often used as a way of avoiding the tough process of hard negotiations. Unfortunately, in bringing in outsiders, negotiators bypass the positive aspects of reaching a mutual agreement on their own. There are, however, instances when it is the only way to move forward, and I have used it over the years. A publicly unpopular strike that neither side wants might be avoided with outside intervention. There are also certain disputes that are tailor-made for TPI. The emotionally charged negotiations involving sexual harassment and divorce lend themselves to this approach as an alternative to lengthy and expensive settlements in court.

Still, I remain a reluctant user of TPI. I am first and foremost a negotiator and do not willingly abdicate my position to a third party.

TYPES OF THIRD-PARTY INTERVENTION

In the popular mind, the various types and definitions of TPI are often confused. Arbitration and its various forms, such as binding arbitration, last-offer binding arbitration, and mediation leading into arbitration, are technical and professional terms. The media will often confuse matters by defining mediation as arbitration, and vice versa. Yet it is crucial to understand the variations, particularly since TPI is becoming more common in marital difficulties, job-related problems, and consumer disputes.

Mediation is *not* arbitration. In mediation, the parties have to agree to the solution. The third party's success is largely determined by its ability to win the confidence of the participants. First, the mediator gives an objective assessment of each side's strengths and weaknesses. Then, the mediator gently guides the parties toward agreement and continues to do so until an agreement is reached.

Arbitration leaves agreement outside the negotiators' hands. The arbitrator determines the agreement based on the facts presented by each side. Unlike the mediator who facilitates negotiation and the solution, the arbitrator dictates the solution.

The Role of the Mediator

I consider mediation the most helpful form of TPI. The mediator is there to move negotiations along and keep the parties talking. The mediator is a bridge, an instrument to the solution. This does not mean the mediator cannot or should not help in bringing about the solution. Ideally, the mediator will position the adversaries so that they keep talking and come to a positive conclusion on their own. Mediation, the least severe form of intervention, is nevertheless quite difficult. The mediators keep the parties talking and calm frayed nerves. They are the peacemakers. They are called in because the adversaries are antagonistic and troubled by each other's solutions, or lack thereof.

The mediator has to be almost faceless. He or she should seek no credit. The mediator's satisfaction comes from obtaining a solution through (and by) the parties. In everyday mediation, the key is to try to find a formula that can be successfully repeated. For example, the parent attempting to quiet an argument when one child wants to watch a baseball game on television and the other wants to watch cartoons ideally will find a way to allocate viewing time between the children now and in the future. This mediation may teach the children to negotiate and resolve this problem or a similar one on their own. The formula can be as simple as agreeing to take turns and keeping to this rule. Once the criteria are established, it is up to the negotiating parties—in this case, the children—to settle future disputes.

In the professional arena, the mediator should have the same goal of focusing on the negotiators and keeping the negotiations going while remaining in the background.

When I first arrived in New York some thirty years ago, Theodore Kheel was considered the preeminent mediator. He was intelligent, authoritative, and above all, popular. Both management and labor reached out to him to mediate. But in reaching out to him, you paid a price.

The price was very simple—the negotiators effectively gave up their seats at the bargaining table, and he took over. The spotlight was on this brilliant man who found the solutions. For me, this type of mediation was especially difficult, and I never called on Ted Kheel.

One famous incident involved Kheel, Mike Quill, the colorful, charismatic leader of the Transit Workers, and Mayor Wagner. A transit strike was in the offing, and the public had much to lose. A transit workers strike is not a simple matter in New York, where the public depends heavily on public transportation. Business would suffer; commercial activity would diminish and would affect the economy.

On this occasion, negotiations deadlocked, and Kheel was brought in. After all-night talks, an unshaven Ted Kheel emerged with his two partners, Wagner and Quill, to announce that a settlement had been reached. There was a municipal sigh of relief. People congratulated each other. In fact, Quill and Wagner set up the situation so that Kheel could finish the negotiations.

Eric Schmertz was almost flawless as a mediator. He was one of the best problem solvers I knew. He had an uncanny ability to make the adversaries keep their eyes on the ball. He had a wonderfully disarming personality and could make you be introspective, make you look hard at yourself. Somehow he knew how to go into troubled waters and calm everybody. He was one of the best mediators we had. But Ed Koch didn't like him.

Ed Koch didn't like mediators in general. Ed was tough, he was opinionated, and nobody knew the truth like Ed did. In all fairness to Ed, he was correct in his assertion that a mediator was a part of reaching the decision. Koch was wary of this involvement, and so he never came across a mediator he really liked.

In fact, it was Ed who put the skids on Ted Kheel. Ted, had become a fixture at the Metropolitan Transit Authority. Koch removed him as the Transit Authority's mediator.

The union, with Ted's urging, fought to keep him on. I believe this was a grave mistake. You cannot have constructive mediation unless both parties have faith in the mediator. Although the mayor is ostensibly not the chief negotiator at the Transit Authority, he has tremendous influence and a huge stake in the outcome. Given Koch's disapproval of him, Kheel had to go. You can fault Ed, but you can't kid yourself: unless both labor and management want the mediator to continue, he can't carry on.

Agreement between the parties to mediate, and agreement on the mediator are also key principles in everyday negotiations. In the following example, these principles were critical to a successful outcome.

When staff cuts were implemented, the senior manager overseeing a small public agency office felt that the only way to handle the workload effectively would be to assign two midlevel managers as co-directors. Neither one could handle the demands of the office alone. Each had his own strengths; one was more technically proficient, the other a stronger administrator. Both types of skills were needed to run the office.

When the senior manager approached these two individuals with the concept that they be co-directors, they enthusiastically accepted. As they proceeded to discuss their individual responsibilities, it soon became clear that there would be some overlap in responsibilities, as well as some potential conflicts: Who would use the director's office? Who would have use of the office vehicle? Who would the subordinate staff report to?

The senior manager suggested that they develop a plan for resolving these types of conflicts. The two individuals were not only colleagues; they were friends who had been classmates in college and saw each other socially. The senior manager did not want their new assignments to interfere with a very good relationship. She had decided to make them co-directors because she felt they could work well together.

They came back to her with a plan. "We want you to be our mediator. When we can't resolve our problems, we want an opportunity to discuss our individual points of view openly and get your opinion."

The senior manager then asked, "Do you want me to make the decisions?" "No," they answered, "but we want your opinion. We also want a commitment from you that in these situations, you will speak to us together, not one-on-one."

The senior manager agreed. The co-directors are doing a great job. They were wise to acknowledge the need for mediation and agree on a mediator and on the criteria for mediation before problems arose. The co-directors called on their mediator fairly often during the first few months. Their need for mediation gradually diminished and now occurs rarely. This is mediation at its best.

Readiness Is Everything

I cannot overemphasize that both sides must not only accept the mediator, but that they must be open to the mediation process. Regardless of the skill of the mediator and the demands of the public, the mediator cannot succeed where there is little or no cooperation by the combatants. At a minimum, the parties must be open to compromise in order to create an environment conducive to success.

In 1994 President Clinton and Secretary of Labor Robert Reich asked Bill Usery, a well-known mediator, to try to mediate the baseball strike. In a recent book, Reich said that he was reluctant to enter the baseball strike, but the president pushed him into it. The baseball owners wanted a complete victory over the ballplayers union. This is exactly the kind of situation that mediation cannot resolve. Usery's efforts were fruitless.

Labor and management must agree to the intervention since either side can destroy the mediator's effectiveness. When this openness doesn't exist, the outcome can border on the tragic. This was the situation in a much-publicized case involving the board of the Andy Warhol Foundation and a friend of mine, a well-known lawyer named Ed Hayes.

A disastrous court case that was costly to all involved ensued between Ed and the foundation board. This case was not only materially costly, but the publicity was counterproductive. It should have been decided out of court. Mediation or arbitration was a positive way out.

The difficulty centered on a contractual fee for Hayes's services, based on a percentage of the worth of the foundation's assets. The board felt it was exorbitant; Ed believed it was due to him on a contractual basis. Objectivity was lost in the growing animosity of the adversaries. The anger escalated in direct proportion to the legal costs of the case.

I knew Ed and some of the board members. Ed believed that he had a solid case. I advised him to accept mediation to resolve the situation. At first, he was adamant. The facts favored him. Why bend?

Without going into the merits of the case, I pointed out that the bad publicity was not helpful to anyone. And going to court would be costly. After some discussion, he agreed to mediation.

I then spoke to a friend on the board. He was furious at Ed and would not consider mediation. I tried to calm him by explaining that you don't negotiate or mediate with friends, then fell back on my own expertise: "You don't have to love your adversary; the major point is to make for a damn settlement." He was obdurate. I lost the argument.

The dispute went to court, and the case was initially settled in Ed's favor. The legal costs were astronomical. My friend on the board, usually an objective, intelligent man, allowed his feelings to overcome his judgment. Emotion overrode reason.

The appellate court then overturned the original decision. Ed has taken a financial beating. The foundation board feels delighted and exonerated, but they have paid astronomical legal costs and reaped unfavorable publicity. Even with the decision in their favor, I bet that mediation would have been more economical.

The case is still in the courts. It is like a game of Ping-Pong. Only the lawyers can win now.

There is great potential for the use of mediation in divorce proceedings and, here too, readiness is everything. We never think about a breakdown in a divorce settlement as a strike, even though, it has all the characteristics of a strike. The party that walks away from an agreement does so with bitterness that makes for a break in the divorce negotiations and creates an atmosphere of rancor when the negotiations continue, much the same as in a strike.

Two friends were locked in divorce proceedings. The man wanted out and took the walk. He was fairly well to do, and the material offer he made seemed adequate to the lawyers. She was justifiably concerned about some key points in the proposed settlement. Some of the clauses allowed for continued control by the husband. Instead of working through these points, she tried to blow up the whole settlement. It became a quasi-public war and nobody benefited.

When she finally agreed to bring in a mediator, the contentious issues were resolved through objective analysis. For example, as part of the initial settlement, the woman had use of the country home. However, her husband insisted on having something to say in how the property was used—for example, whether she could rent it or who her guests could be.

The mediator was able to persuade the woman that her husband's concern was based on the fact that the property eventually would go to their children. His intent was not to control her, but to protect his children's future property. The mediator proposed that the husband relinquish his right of approval on how the property would be used in exchange for the responsibility of the wife to remedy any damages to the house or property.

Robert Cohen, a top divorce lawyer, observes that people in his field must deal with human beings in a highly charged, angry atmosphere. In some cases, Cohen insists, divorce lawyers are merely messengers. In other cases, they have to take complete control, counseling clients on every aspect of the settlement, even negotiating the settlement. Cohen believes in mediation if the adversaries are ready, but feels that this readiness is rare.

Cohen contends that there is a major difference between divorce negotiations and other professional negotiations. Divorce negotiations can drag on for years. The anger and vindictiveness of one party or both can lead to disruptions, delays, and seemingly eternal haggling. In other types of negotiations, Cohen believes, the parties are more interested in a settlement, regardless of the animosity. Not so with divorce.

My own divorce took almost three years. Cohen assured me that this was relatively brief compared to some of the divorces he has handled. Some have lasted five to ten years.

Custody of the children in a divorce is one issue that is perfect for mediation. More often than not, the children are the main victims of divorce. Because I could not communicate with my wife, Sarah, during the divorce negotiations, we were unable to minimize the tension and the pain of breaking up. Obviously, this was terrible for the children.

My ex-wife was given custody of our daughter, but Rachel did not want to live with her mother. Legal pressure was put on me to relinquish custody of her. To the best of my knowledge, nobody spoke to Rachel. I conceded. It was a mistake. Rachel left Sarah at the age of sixteen, bitter and unhappy, and came to live with Betsy and me. We had a difficult child on our hands. Things eventually turned out well thanks to Betsy's sensitivity and Rachel's positive response.

Mediators should be used in conjunction with divorce lawyers, especially for issues involving children. While it's hard for me to imagine mediation working in my own divorce, it couldn't have hurt. It may not save time or money in the short term, but it could ameliorate the impact of the divorce on the children in the long term.

Other types of personal disputes lend themselves to TPI. Sexual harassment, and race, age, and gender descrimination charges may be prime candidates.

Premature Mediation

As a labor leader, I insisted on the right to strike, but used this weapon only rarely. In any strike, the media beat the hell out of the union, and the public blames the union for the hardship and inconvenience it suffers.

The growing negative attitude toward strikes led to an increase in the use of alternative dispute resolution, something I believe to be counterproductive. Labor leaders are so concerned about avoiding strikes that negotiations are prematurely aborted in favor of TPI.

This is the case with the Railway Labor Act. The law, created to avoid strikes, leads both sides to an early impasse, followed by TPI. The negotiating process is reduced to a minor activity, when it should be the major process for dispute resolution. The immediate dispute may be resolved by TPI, but negative relations linger on. There is no real therapy.

The continuing battle between labor and management of the Long Island Railroad is an example of how TPI can stifle real progress. Bruce McIver, in his capacity as CEO and chief negotiator for the Long Island Railroad, had to operate under the Railway Labor Act. He found it duplicative, frustrating, and regressive and gave as a compelling example what he called the "incident" of 1985.

The largest and most powerful local, the United Transport Workers Union, was headed by Eddie Yule. Early in the negotiations, with the help of federal mediation, Yule agreed to a settlement. This would set the stage for settlements with the other unions. Regrettably, the time allowances provided by the Railway Labor Act also give the negotiators an opportunity to play games. The long, drawn-out process becomes part of the negotiations. The act mandates a sixty-day mediation period to cool off, a ninety-day period for consideration by an emergency board created by the labor act, and a sixty-day decision-making period for the emergency board.

At the end of this period in 1985, the unions that hadn't settled went out on strike. After eleven days, Congress imposed a settlement. To nobody's surprise, it was identical to the original one recommended by the emergency board.

This convoluted attempt to preclude strikes has the opposite effect. A period of time can't resolve issues; only negotiations can. The mandatory cooling-off period is at best ineffective; at worst, it totally backfires.

I often say, show me a strike-free society, and I will show you an authoritarian government. Strikes were forbidden in Stalin's Soviet Union and in Hitler's Germany. If strikes are forbidden, then mediation is useless. Why settle if you have the upper hand? The threat of a strike is a compelling reason for management to settle. It can be a leveling factor for both sides since both sides can be hurt by a strike.

In determining whether to go to mediation, and when to do so, it is important to consider all of those who will be affected by the outcome. In particular, when the mediated agreement is a pattern setter, a premature decision can be costly, as it was in a negotiation involving the Teamsters Union and the Dinkins administration.

The Teamsters were in a weak position in their contract talks. The timing was such that if they settled, the other unions would be equally weakened, despite their stronger positions. I therefore urged the head of the Teamsters to hold back and delay the talks until the other unions settled. Instead, the head of the union went into mediation. What a disaster! The mediated settlement, a percentage point below my benchmark, now set the pattern and left the other unions helpless. Mediation would be useless since no mediator could allow for a higher settlement than the previous one. A strike was out of the question since it would be viewed as undermining the Teamsters. In this case, premature mediation badly hurt thousands of other workers.

Successful Mediation

A firehouse was to be eliminated as a cost-saving item for New York City. Mayor Abe Beame insisted the firehouse was not needed. Similar response time to any fire in the community could be guaranteed by other firehouses, he said. The community was irate. They held the firehouse hostage, taking it over in a sit-in.

The majority of dwellings in this community were wood-frame homes, extremely vulnerable to fire. The leadership of the community was united. The mayor called for mediation. Basil Paterson, an expert in community and labor relations, was called in.

Basil was sympathetic to the mayor's needs. Mediators need to neutralize the situation, but this should not mean that they have neutral feelings. Mediators can have more sensitivity to the needs of one of the parties. In this case, Basil felt that government was exercising a legitimate right.

The adversaries disliked each other. John O'Hagan, a tough and seasoned fire officer, was negotiating for the city. Adam Veneski, equally tough and dedicated to his community, was negotiating on the other side. Sparks continued to fly. In this case, Basil, a mild-mannered, intelligent mediator, was perfect. Through personal attention and honest concern, he kept both sides friendly to him, if not to each other.

The community leadership brought in witnesses with excellent credentials, including a former officer in the Fire Department. The witnesses from the community were articulate people with exceptionally well-reasoned arguments. The city, for its part, switched arguments. It no longer talked of cost savings, but now emphasized response time. It built its case on maintaining community safety.

The animosity had diminished, and Basil felt it was time to bring both sides together. Since a settlement seemed possible, Basil informed both groups that he wanted an immediate meeting and a solution. O'Hagan had a wedding to attend that day, but Basil felt any delay would hurt. Timing is extremely important in a resolution. O'Hagan came to the meeting immediately after the wedding, at 11:00 P.M.

By 6:30 A.M., a settlement had been reached. The firehouse would remain open but with less equipment and manpower. Both sides grumbled a bit, but Basil could sense they were not totally unhappy. Since even mediators have egos, Basil was satisfied with the outcome and deserved the credit.

He was the quintessential mediator. He knew when to bring the parties together. He cooled the heated antagonisms. His timing for a solution was excellent. Above all, he obtained a solution both sides could agree to.

Mediation has been most appropriately and successfully used in the workplace with individual grievances, contractual disagreements, and day-to-day conflicts, as in the example that follows.

A major magazine had recruited a talented and successful editor. She had signed a contract that addressed wages and benefits, and included a noncompete clause for two years after leaving the magazine. Her involvement in editorial and work assignments was not clearly spelled out in the contract, and she was increasingly disappointed in her assignments. In addition, she believed that the publisher was a sexist. The situation grew worse.

After nine months on the job, she sued the publisher. She demanded elimination of the noncompete clause and $75,000 in damages.

Her lawyer recommended mediation. Court cases were expensive. Both sides agreed to mediation.

Although the woman wanted some money, she was incensed about the noncompete clause. She felt the publisher was dishonest and demeaning. She wanted out and wanted to get on with her professional life. The publisher's lawyer was adamant on both counts: no money and perhaps only a minor change in the noncompete clause.

The mediator kept the adversaries in different rooms. He found it more helpful to deal with their lawyers. His approach was time-consuming, but it was working.

Since the woman wanted to get on with her life, he had the publisher loosen up on the noncompete clause. At the same time, the woman lowered her severance demands. He reached a point where the noncompete clause was down to three months and the severance was down to $15,000. Like most other mediation cases, he reached a fairly good level of settlement, but then intransigence set in on one minor point.

On the final offer from the publisher, elimination of the noncompete clause with no severance, the mediator brought in the lawyers for both sides. The lawyer representing the woman underscored that she wanted some compensation The other side insisted they would eliminate the noncompete clause only without paying any money.

Most mediators have the sense to know when they have a settlement at hand. He recommended three months and $7,500. The publisher's lawyer insisted it was not the money but the principle.

The mediator was adept at this kind of situation. Did the publisher really need for this situation to get out of hand because of some monetary compensation? Couldn't they take as a face-saving solution a settlement of the claims at 90 percent less than the original demand?

The publisher reluctantly agreed. The woman was satisfied. The mediator handled the case exceptionally well. He knew when to be firm. As happened here, usually one side or the other will concede when the settlement is close.

Arbitration

In arbitration, the judicial process is paramount. Once the arbitrator is selected by a judge, neither side can remove him, as they can a mediator. Nevertheless, an arbitrator, like a mediator, should have the confidence of both sides. It is imperative that an arbitrator not be imposed on either side.

Arbitration is meaningless if the decision is not binding, as in a court of law. Once a judge makes a decision, it must be carried out. The arbitration arena and procedures are much more rigid and confining than those associated with mediation. A meeting room is established, witnesses are called in, and documentation is presented. The arbitrator is similar to a judge in that he or she can meet with any of the adversaries outside the room (or courtroom). The arbitrator can sound out the adversaries on what they will accept. Although the arbitrator's decision is binding, he is sensitive to the needs of the combatants. This makes for a major difference with a judge.

Because of the arbitrator's strength, each side is careful about its behavior. You worry less about alienating a mediator since his decision is not binding. The arbitrator will make a final decision. But unlike a judge, an arbitrator must worry about obtaining more assignments. In other words, he is dependent on those he has served to obtain future work.

Arbitrators, like judges, become known by their decisions. My general counsel at the union, Bev Gross, kept a dossier on arbitrators. Today there are more women arbitrators. They are expected to bring an increased sensitivity and empathy to cases involving women.

Never allow your adversary to select the arbitrator. Do plenty of research on the subject. Hire lawyers or people knowledgeable about the reputations of arbitrators. A poor selection can be a disaster.

Above all, try to avoid arbitration. If a dispute cannot be settled through negotiations, then pursue mediation. This allows you a larger role than arbitration.

Arbitration does have its place, particularly in circumstances under which you may be too powerful—where your strength can become unwieldy. For example, the union I represented controlled the water supply of New York City. We could go on strike and shut it down. We could create such havoc by striking that the reputation of the union itself might be destroyed. So in circumstances of this nature, arbitration was preferable to a strike. The police and fire departments are in the same situation. They wanted impartial arbitration since they knew that it was almost impossible for them to strike.

If a negotiator is in a position of weakness or lacks the strike weapon, arbitration may be a good solution. Arbitration would have been an excellent alternative to the overwhelming strength of the Daley administration when I was in Chicago. But we never received the right to arbitrate. Daley was no dummy. Why give up power?

Selecting an Arbitrator

The process of selecting an arbitrator is the same in the public sector and the private sector. The selection sets the tone and is key to the outcome. It is crucial that you make sure the arbitration will be impartial. This can be somewhat tricky. Management may come forth with a list of impartial arbitrators. The list may look quite good. The problem is that once someone decides who's on the list, impartiality is questionable. We had this difficulty with the Public Employee Relations Board.

The governor selected the impartials. Were they good people? In the main, they were excellent. However, the governor selected them, and those whom the governor anoints, he can dismiss. They serve at the pleasure of the governor. Whoever controls the arbitration procedure, controls the negotiations.

In all fairness, the Public Employee Relations Board operated very well in the years that I was around. Governors Carey and Cuomo were decent men. I don't know how it functions under a conservative governor such as George Pataki.

There is a simple solution to the problem of who selects the arbitrator—the American Arbitration Association. The association thrives because of a reputation for impartiality. It has a procedure where both parties make the decision on the choice of an arbitrator.

Again, my strong preference is for the parties to try to settle issues themselves, through private negotiations. Beyond the specific settlements, the traditional negotiations process can result in longer-term understanding among the parties, or what I call therapy for both sides.

Arbitrating for Cover

The head of a department in a large paint factory was African American. His number-two person was an aggressive and idealistic Hispanic who seemed more concerned about Cuba than about his job. He would sometimes take days off, without notifying his superior.

There was ethnic sensitivity. A large part of the workforce in the factory was Hispanic. The number-two person was considered a hero, but to the top man, the situation had become impossible. Nevertheless, he was reluctant to fire the man.

His procrastination only worsened the situation. The animosity flowed over into the workforce. The department head's refusal to treat the matter professionally brought about the very situation he

hoped to avoid, and the Hispanic workers staged a sit-in. Since neither man belonged to the union, the factory management inter-
vened. At this point, it wanted a judicial settlement. Arbitration
would insulate management from criticism. It would give them a
cover. They brought in the American Arbitration Association, and
an arbitrator was selected.

The situation was difficult. Besides procrastinating, the supervisor had made additional mistakes. He had nothing on the record.
He had gone from acquiescence in the number two's behavior to
verbal resentment, then, threats to dismiss him.

On the other hand, the supervisor's desire to get rid of this subordinate was justified. The man had clearly defied supervision, and
he had a terrible case. The major error was that the supervisor had
put nothing on the record.

The arbitrator was provided with workers as witnesses. He spent
a great deal of time talking to both parties and reading up on personnel policies. In talking to the number-two man, he found a person who was oblivious to his faults. But the supervisor had never
documented and discussed these faults.

The arbitrator decided that:

- The number-two person was to be transferred to another part
  of the factory.
- A negative analysis of his behavior became part of the record.
- Any further abuse on his part would be immediate cause for
  dismissal.
- The supervisor was criticized for his delay in using his authority. The major criticism of him was his lack of documentation
  and failure to define for the man his violation of work ethics.

The arbitrator acknowledged his concern over the ethnic rivalry.
A tough decision could poison relations in the plant. He also believed the number-two person was unaware of the consequences
of his behavior. Consequently, the error of his work ethic was
detailed in the report. The arbitrator made certain the man knew

that transfer was his last chance in remaining on the job.

The arbitrator's decision was final, which put him in a stronger position. He could only hope that all sides learned a lesson from the incident.

Last-Offer Binding Arbitration

Last-offer binding arbitration (LOBA) is even more judicial than arbitration itself. It gives the arbitrator very little leeway. LOBA is exactly what it sounds like: a last offer is made by both parties, and the arbitrator selects the final offer of one of the parties. There is no negotiation. Both sides have to live with that decision. There is no flexibility.

LOBA has been adopted by the baseball union and baseball management, and I believe it's one of the reasons that relations have been difficult between these two parties. LOBA is really a statement to one side that it lost. But it does serve a purpose. When the parties are far apart, LOBA forces them to move. It says, in effect, "Okay, now at least you'll give me final offers." This imposes real discipline on the parties. Since one of the two figures will be selected, each side is forced to move close to what it thinks is a reasonable offer. I think it is too disciplined, too restrictive. It takes too much away from the negotiations process.

I don't recommend LOBA for individuals involved in private negotiations. Unlike the other forms of TPI, LOBA is too one-sided for private disputes.

Remember the Goal

If you want to keep something out of court or out of the public eye, whether it's a divorce with custody or a sexual harassment suit, I recommend mediation or arbitration. Either one can be a positive alternative to the traditional court battles where often the

lawyers are the only winners. I continue to believe that direct negotiation between the two parties is still the most positive way of
resolving differences.

Most experts who discuss the subject talk about win-win situations. More often than not, it's hard to identify the winner. It is
much more important that, after agreement has finally been
reached, people get on with the business of positive relations and
positive living, and dispose of the acrimony, the antagonisms, the
disagreements that led up to the negotiations. I believe that all
these are resolvable within the framework of negotiations. That
way both sides can walk away and feel it's over with. It's over with
because we agreed to the solution.

It is of paramount importance that TPI lead to a solution. Both
parties must be ready to take the step toward outside help and
must agree on its form and the intermediaries. The best mediator is
the professional who obtains a solution from the parties. This is the
goal and should remain so from the start through completion.

As much as possible, the disagreement should be kept out of the
press. This is difficult where the participants have high personal
visibility. The mediator should have no visibility.

If you are a clear winner, keep your mouth shut. There is no
need to state the obvious. Good third-party professionals will request their clients to be discreet. Even the angriest of antagonists
may find themselves involved with one another again someday.
It's nicer to allow everybody to live for another day.

Chapter Eight

NEGOTIATIONS THAT FAILED—AND WHY

Best-sellers such as *Getting to Yes* would have you believe that negotiations should always lead to win-win solutions. Other popular books state with conviction that you will never have to lose an argument. After my almost thirty-five years as a negotiator, there is something of which I am certain—there are negotiations with losers. There are negotiations that become difficult for both sides, and both sides take a terrible beating.

In the real world, even highly professional, experienced negotiators can sometimes find themselves in losing situations. Sometimes these failures are not due to a lack of preparation or a failure to assess an adversary or a violation of other basic principles of negotiation. But more often than not, they are. When there is a breakdown, it is usually due to one of the following breaches in the basic principles of negotiating: noncommunication, excessive emotional involvement, or underestimating your adversary.

Losing does have one saving grace: we can learn and grow from the experience. Given the clarity of hindsight, we can understand that in most failed negotiations, failure could have been avoided.

I use as examples two very different negotiations. The 1994 major league baseball strike was of national significance, yet noncommunication doomed the negotiations; and in my own divorce, my emotional involvement negated my experience as a negotiator and even caused me to forget some of my own principles of negotiation.

Noncommunication and excessive emotional involvement are two common reasons for failure. They happen every day to everyone. They erode the negotiations process and make the negotiations futile.

In Chapter 5 I cited the negotiations during the 1974 New York City fiscal crisis to demonstrate the successful implementation of the principles I advocate. In the next two examples I show what happened when one or more of the basic principles was ignored.

THE BASEBALL STRIKE OF 1994

The essence of this strike is quite simple and quite straightforward. The owners of the major league teams had a bottom line: a salary cap. In effect, it was an ultimatum, a nonnegotiable issue; and this, in and of itself, represents the first breach in the basic principles.

You Cannot Negotiate an Ultimatum

Although the insistence on a salary cap was only one aspect of the noncommunication that led to the strike, it should have given a loud and clear signal of the impasse to come.

The salary cap would dictate a specific amount of spending for each club. The rationale for this was that those clubs that were losing money or making only marginal profits suffered in their ability to attract and compensate the best players. The argument was that if there were no salary cap, the stronger clubs—the moneyed clubs—could buy the superior players and continue to augment their strength. From the very beginning, the baseball owners insisted that the salary cap was a nonnegotiable issue. Some took a hard line.

The players' union believed that the players were subsidizing the less profitable ball clubs. Management insisted that the way to equalize profits was by capping salaries Yet management had no cap on profits. Why couldn't there be a redistribution of profits? In effect, management was forcing the players to accept a responsibility that the players believed management should have worked out among themselves.

Whom Do You Represent, and What Are the Needs?

Although only six of the clubs wanted to negotiate, the majority group imposed a ruling that made it impossible for the minority group to have a real voice. The rule required that a three-quarters majority of owners would need to be in agreement to implement a policy. In fact, the minority owners, the doves, were isolated. They had very little say in the negotiations. Richard Ravitch, who headed the negotiations for the owners, could hardly deal with the minority group at all.

In the September 18, 1994, *New York Times,* Pat Jordan reports that Peter Angelos, owner of the Baltimore Orioles, and a dove in the dispute, told Ravitch that the players had some legitimate arguments and that Angelos asked Ravitch to provide a detailed analysis of the negotiations to the players. Ravitch refused. Angelos felt that "based on a balanced, rational approach to the owner-player impasse, there could be resolution." Both Ravitch and Donald Fehr, the players' representative, made for very poor public figures. They appeared humorless, obdurate, and unable to communicate their arguments. To be fair, they were only the messengers, representing the owners and the players. The problem, as I mentioned, was that Ravitch was not representing all the owners. In truth, Ravitch had no elbow room. The hard-core owners boxed him in. Ravitch, an experienced negotiator, could not use his expertise. He took a bad rap for this. The hawk owners wanted it their way or no way; they were offering an ultimatum. They put

Ravitch in an impossible position, which was inconsistent with his experience and intelligence. The result was that the dove owners felt that Ravitch and the hawk owners were intentionally alienating them.

This is an important policy issue in negotiations. Those antagonistic to the chief negotiator must be treated with sensitivity. The doves accepted the proposition of unity at the bargaining table and in the media. In a very real sense, they kept their part in the negotiations above board. The place for dissent is behind the scenes and in caucuses. This is a key point in negotiations. Such disagreements must be worked out privately so that there can be public unity.

Negotiations are hardly ever unanimous. The minority may be totally opposed to the majority or may have only misgivings. There can be anything in between. But whatever the nature of the opposition, attention must be paid.

A couple is bargaining for a house. One of the partners is concerned about the price. The other partner may be ready to pay more because he wants the house and has a fear of losing it. This should be worked out privately before making or raising an offer.

Differences must not be brought to the field of battle. The negotiations should reflect your group's unity. The best way to achieve this is to talk out disagreements behind the scenes. In the baseball negotiations, the media picked up the fact that the minority owners' group was unhappy. This could have been avoided if attention were paid to the doves.

As chief negotiator, Ravitch was probably forced to go along with the majority owners. In doing so, he became alienated from the doves. The conversation with Angelos, as reported, was evidence that Ravitch, was not an ameliorative factor among his own constituents, the group he had to represent. Instead, he was forced to carry a message generated by the hawks, contributing to the tension and the divisions.

The chief negotiator for the players, Donald Fehr, seemed passive and cavalier. Fehr's demeanor gave the impression that he represented only the multimillionaires among the baseball players. This was not so, but Fehr lost an opportunity to demonstrate his sensitivity to the fans, who, after all, were the real victims of the strike.

The Stakeholders Not at the Table

The general public and the fans in particular, who are the real clients, were not represented in these negotiations.

Dick Ravitch, in an interview in *Newsday*, insisted baseball is a business. One might not argue with that, but if it is a business, shouldn't it be concerned about its clients? During the entire interview, Ravitch, as the owners' representative, showed little sensitivity to the men, women, and children who pay their way into the ballpark. The American public seemed to have no say in the drama that was taking place at the bargaining table even though baseball is America's national pastime. In all of these negotiations, the public should have been of deep concern to the participants. This was a terrible error of omission, but only one of the unusual aspects of these negotiations. The talks were sporadic and counterproductive. Neither side stayed at the bargaining table. Each would make offers, then disappear, then return when a counteroffer was made. This is not negotiating.

The long, drawn-out periods of silence only worsened the frustration that the public felt. The baseball season was going down the drain as the two sides failed to resolve their disagreements.

Such public animosity is not unusual. Nobody loves a strike. Even though one might fault the owners for their nonnegotiating tactics, the public usually blames the people walking on the picket line—those who are holding back their services. This is a fact I often remind my labor colleagues of. A strike never makes the public happy, and that is something that regrettably must be lived with.

During dinners with my friends Fred and Judy Wilpon, I usually avoided talking about the strike. Fred Wilpon is the major owner of the New York Mets. I knew the subject was painful for Fred, and being a team player, he wasn't going to divulge anything to me. However, I couldn't resist telling him that I was amazed by the negotiations, specifically by the fact that the parties were not staying at the table and torturing each other into looking for a way out. It confused and upset me, and I couldn't figure it out. Fred's only response was, "Victor, these are not your kind of negotiations." I didn't respond because I wouldn't put Fred in an awkward situation. But I thought to myself, Neither are they yours, Fred.

Third-Party Intervention

There was no movement at the bargaining table, but there was movement at the National Labor Relations Board (NLRB) and in the courts. The unions filed an unfair management practice petition against the owners. The substance of their argument was since there really was no impasse, management had no right to negate two of the more important parts of the union's contract: salary arbitration and the free agency clause. The free agency clause defined the right of players with six years' seniority to negotiate their services with another club. The National Labor Relations Board agreed with the players and upheld these two clauses since an impasse had not been reached or agreed on. This decision was upheld by the U.S. Court of Appeals for the Second Circuit. In its ruling, the court made an important but little publicized statement which, in essence, said: "This strike has captivated the public's attention. Given the popularity of the sport as well as the protracted nature and well documented bitterness of the strike, [this strike] is about more than just whether the players and the owners will resolve their differences."

The NLRB ruling and the court decision brought the strike to an end. The doves became vocal. Fred Wilpon let it be known in a statement to *The New York Times* that he was going to lobby to make certain the judicial decisions were carried out and that play resumed. The players voted to go back to work, and management did not lock them out.

Baseball cannot afford another strike. Management suffered financially during and after the strike. Even when games resumed, advertising revenue decreased, as did attendance at the ballparks. In some cases, ticket prices had to be lowered. Eventually enthusiasm began to revive, and people were paying attention to baseball again.

Negotiations between owners and players resumed, but Dick Ravitch—who in my opinion was more a victim than a perpetrator—was replaced by Randy Levine, Mayor Giuliani's chief negotiator.

As head of negotiations for the Giuliani administration, Randy Levine had demonstrated exceptional skill. He communicated with unions. He did this not only at the bargaining table but at union meetings and educational conferences. He was known to the union leaders. He was flexible and sensitive.

He conducted himself the same way in the baseball negotiations. Fehr became more relaxed. He found it easier to deal with Randy Levine. The fact the dove owners were now participating was of major significance. This became painfully apparent after an agreement was reached between Levine and Fehr.

Much to everybody's astonishment, the owners balked at the tentative agreement. This seemed unbelievable because as those of us professionals in negotiating knew, the tentative agreement could not have been reached without the owners' approval, at least not without the approval of their chosen spokesman, owner Bud Selig. He had hired and supported Levine. Then these strange negotiations took another bizarre twist.

The owner of the Chicago White Sox, Jerry Reinsdorf, a leading hawk who insisted on a salary cap for the players, gave Albert

Belle, his top player, an astronomical salary agreement. The press excoriated him, and the doves seized the moment. They came to Randy Levine's aid. Bud Selig, who had undermined Levine, only to be undone by Reinsdorf's action, was forced to back the agreement Levine and Fehr had reached. A satisfactory long-range contract was signed.

So many basic principles of negotiating were violated in the baseball strike that it is a textbook example of how not to negotiate. Here is another.

MY DIVORCE

In recounting my own failure as a negotiator during my divorce I'm not trying to justify my actions or criticize my ex-wife's actions or reactions. Although it would be easy to indulge myself, it is far more important to document, as objectively as possible, the difficulties of divorce and what happened to my negotiating principles in the process. First, some background . . .

I met my wife, Betsy, in 1974 at the New York State Democratic Party Convention. I had been married to Sarah for more than thirty years, and, to put it mildly, my marriage was in trouble. But part from my marriage, life was very good and very exciting. We had four great kids, my job kept me busy and productive, and my position in the New York City community was both secure and rewarding. Although the home fires were no longer burning, I did not feel driven to leave, and we kept the marriage going. There had been some women in the past, but those relationships were not deep. None of those women had the impact on me that Betsy had.

Betsy became an important part of my life. Our relationship was so close and important that I made up my mind we were going to get married.

The Power Position

I soon discovered that by virtue of being the spouse who wanted out, I was automatically in a weaker negotiating position than Sarah. No matter how you sliced it, the divorce was my fault. Sarah was the victim, and I was the bad guy. I would have to pay for it. Sarah was in the power position.

With one strike already against me, another overwhelming handicap was my overriding concern for the children. I compensated by worrying about all of them and trying to insulate them from the divorce. My two oldest could handle it. They had the maturity and strength to absorb the emotional shock. My daughter, Rachel, was in a more difficult position. She was quite young, and her relationship with her mother, as with many other twelve-year-old girls, was strained. The worst part was that Rachel believed that I was leaving Momma *and* her. Oddly enough, she displayed no animosity toward me for leaving Sarah, but she felt isolated and feared that I would neglect her. So I tried hard to allay those fears.

My youngest son, Noah, fifteen at the time, had the biggest difficulty with the breakup and with me. He was not only at a tough, adolescent stage; he was very close to his mother and identified strongly with her. I became the villain, a fact that led me to overcompensate in trying to deal with him. It was an exercise in futility.

My emotional involvement further weakened my ability to negotiate and simultaneously added to Sarah's power.

Because I wanted to remarry, I was driven by this strong emotional need throughout the long period of my divorce. This was yet another emotional complication for me.

The ultimate difficulty was dealing with Sarah. There was absolutely no communication between us. Understandably, she felt victimized and violated. She did not want to talk to me. Thus it became quite easy for me to leave the negotiations to my lawyer. I did explain to my lawyer what my goals were but I left the talks to him. Thinking back, I see it was unfair to him.

My lawyer was a decent man and tried to mollify Sarah, but he was exhausted by the whole process. He met alone with Sarah and her lawyer. I stayed out of it. I did not pay enough attention to my lawyer.

During the process, I used my second son, Irv, as a bellwether to try to address some of the concerns I had regarding the children. He was helpful in this regard, but he was also sensitive to the fact that his mother had the broken wing. He bent over backward to make certain that she would be taken care of. So while he wanted to ensure his mother's well-being, I wanted to be certain that he and the other kids were satisfied. I wasn't participating in the negotiations, and I was overcompensating emotionally with my kids. I would make other mistakes.

No Substitute for Knowledge

I compounded my errors when I allowed Sarah to escalate after she had agreed to a settlement. Whenever we would seem to come to an agreement on an issue, and my lawyer would say to me, "Victor, it looks like it's locked up," I breathed a sigh of relief. But then Sarah would escalate her demands. I should have realized what was happening and gone to court. But then the image of the children would appear in my mind, and I would back down to insulate them from a public battle.

Every time my lawyer and I conceded a point, we went through the same routine again. My worst mistake was agreeing to a cost of living adjustment that I couldn't afford financially. I agreed without even understanding its true cost. I was unprepared, did not know the facts, and breached another basic principle of negotiating.

Confrontation

Just when I thought it was over, the final escalation came into play. I then spoke to my lawyer and said, "We're taking it to court." He looked at me and smiled and said, "I'm glad you've reached that conclusion. I wasn't going to push you into it, but I don't believe you'll have to go." He was right.

Sarah folded. She had a tough, intelligent lawyer, and he knew that she couldn't get as good a deal as she was getting if we went to court.

Emotion Overtakes Intelligence

With a settlement in hand, I added a clause that identified my three sons as arbiters should there be any future difficulties between Sarah and me. What a mistake!

First of all, it was unfair to the kids and involved them unnecessarily. They didn't have to carry this burden. An alternative arbitration procedure should have been put in place.

Emotion, when it overtakes intelligence, wipes out your principles, your logic, your ability to reason. You become a victim of your own feelings, and nobody gains.

As someone pointed out to me, divorce is a different kind of negotiating experience. As in other types of negotiations, however, there is a need for positive involvement—you shouldn't just leave it to the lawyer, even if you have the best lawyer money can buy. I should have taken on a more positive role and dealt with the issues more pragmatically.

It may be easier said than done, but you can't allow your emotions to overtake you. Second, you can't put your intelligence in storage. I complained about the cost of living adjustment I agreed to. I should have looked at it more carefully before agreeing to it, particularly its long-term effects.

Divorce was a learning experience, but I believe I will never have to use the lessons. I told Betsy that if she ever wants to leave me, "Just take everything with you. I can't go through it again." She looks at me sympathetically, as if to say, This poor, pathetic man; I can't leave him. He needs me. I do need you, Betsy, and one divorce in a lifetime is one too many. Betsy's presence and my kids' maturity and growth have more than compensated for a terrible divorce negotiation.

•   •   •

The examples in this chapter share at least one common thread: the breakdowns did not have to happen. Another similarity is that strength did not ensure a positive outcome. The power people played it wrong. They may have been holding the cards, but they played the wrong suit. They had neither sensitivity to the immediate, nor an undertanding of the future implications.

The very best negotiators acknowledge their difficulties and mistakes, and work to rectify their faults. But the trial-and-error approach does not work for everyone. Some people fall into the same pit over and over. That's why you must carefully prepare for negotiations and always follow the basic principles.

Chapter Nine

THE SANCTITY
OF THE CONTRACT

In the United States more than in any other country, a contract is sacred. It is considered a final document by all signers, and its authority is a bedrock principle of American democracy, serving as a protection of our values. It is a protection that gives us social and economic security.

The value Americans place on a contract is evident and seems to be increasing. From prenuptual agreements to living wills, individuals and couples feel the need to get it in writing, and often with good reason. Whether we are seeking to protect an inheritance, property, or other assets, or seeking to assert our right to decide on the degree of extraordinary medical procedures to be administered in the event of a serious illness, contracts give security to the parties involved and to their families.

Even informal transactions may warrant more than a handshake. Furniture delivery dates, cost estimates for small repair work on your home, even commitments between you and your children are strengthened and made more likely to be executed when all parties have signed on the dotted line. Our society has changed. Where mutual trust once ruled, a written agreement may now be required.

In general, I prefer handshake agreements and like to believe that people will keep their word. However, my advice is that if you are suspicious or if you don't know the person with whom you are negotiating, then you need a written contract. For example, the first time you hire a specific contractor to work on your home, you should probably get written cost and schedule estimates. Once you've had a chance to assess the contractor's performance, you may not feel the need in the future to go beyond a verbal agreement.

The increasing popularity of certain types of contractual agreements reflects changes in society. Obviously, with people living longer and with new medical techniques, some people felt the need for living wills and single-page "Do Not Resuscitate" orders. Prenuptual agreements, once thought of for only the extremely wealthy, are now more common among young couples embarking on a first marriage. These agreements can cover everything from distribution of their assets to custody of the pets. Given that these agreements necessarily contemplate the marriage's demise, the negotiations over these agreements must be handled with great sensitivity. There are cases where the negotiations have resulted in abandoning the prenuptual agreement. In other cases, the result was abandoning the planned marriage. Ideally, the couple seeking the agreement are madly in love yet recognize that disagreements about money can be costly to the marriage and the individuals.

A contract documents an agreement. Because of the importance we place on a contract, it is not surprising that negotiations, the process by which we reach the agreement, are often slow and arduous. Once a contract is signed, the expectation is that all parties feel a strong responsibility to comply with its terms. However, the exception can sometimes become the rule. For example, when the economic status of a partner changes after the marriage, prenuptual agreements are often challenged. Then they may have to be renegotiated.

I had a friend whose husband's income soared during their marriage. The prenuptual agreement did not contain an escalation clause. Then her husband wanted out of the marriage and did not want to drag out the separation period. My friend was poised to make a legal challenge. Contractually, she had a weak case, but she had public relations on her side plus her husband's desire to move on, which added to her power.

The solution was a lump-sum payment. He would pay her off and sever the relationship. He made her an offer she couldn't refuse, she accepted, and they went their separate ways. They agreed to discard the contract.

Similarly, when Marla Maples protested over her prenuptual agreement with Donald Trump, the contract took a back seat. Given the brief press coverage of this event, one can only surmise that he must have upped the payment.

In labor relations, after a tedious and difficult battle to win a representation election, management will at times procrastinate and attempt to deny the union a meaningful contract. Negotiations will be prolonged and even subverted. This can be an effective management tactic since the membership is new and insecure, and therefore it is unlikely that the workers will take some militant action. But this delaying strategy demonstrates management's recognition of the sanctity of a contract. While they can deny the workers certain demands along the way, they cannot deny the terms of the ultimate product—a signed contract.

As I mentioned in discussing my divorce, when one party feels at a disadvantage, she or he will prolong the negotiations, even for years. The process of finalizing a divorce can take as long as five to ten years, and it becomes costly in both human and material terms. Those concerned that they will eventually lose can delay indefinitely. Here, lawyers become the key players.

The importance that Americans place on a contract may explain why, on a per capita basis, we have more lawyers in the United States than any other country. (No other country even comes close.) In almost every facet of life, we call on lawyers. During my career in labor and as a labor negotiator, I sought the very best, and I relied on them.

For the most part, a contract can be changed only when both sides agree to that change. If anyone attempts to make a change unilaterally, it is considered a violation of the contract and will not stand up in court if challenged, regardless of the validity of the change. The only way a contract can be changed is through formal contract amendments, mutually agreed to by both sides.

There were two instances during my career where such amendments came about—one that benefited the union and one that benefited management. When we negotiated away severance one year, the older and more powerful members were up in arms and put the union completely on the defensive. To stick to the contract, I would have had to pay a terrible political price. But I could not get a change unless management agreed. They did, which eliminated a great deal of political hardship and enabled me to overcome a very bad mistake in negotiations.

The other example was a change we made on behalf of management when Mayor John Lindsay's chief negotiator, Herb Haber, put a decimal point in the wrong place, costing the city an extra $27 million. There was an interesting twist here. We hadn't yet signed a contract, but Herb respected the agreement reached at the table prior to signing. This was standard practice, as it is in many parts of the business world. Whenever a verbal agreement was reached, we shook hands. It was understood that this agreement would be the basis of the contract, and neither side would change it. We never would reverse ourselves after shaking hands on an agreement.

I take great pride in the fact that every mayor, even the acerbic Mr. Koch, would state that "when Vic made a deal it stuck." I felt the same way about the mayors. This doesn't mean that attempts to alter agreements did not occur. What is important is that unilateral changes were never attempted.

For example, early in Koch's administration, tax revenue diminished unexpectedly, and the mayor had a tough time balancing the city's budget. He called the union leadership to Gracie Mansion to ask for some relief. He did not threaten us or call for punitive actions. He wanted our cooperation. The unions' response was, "No dice." We believed there was a real possibility that the city's economy would improve, and anyway, the mayor had other options if tax revenues continued to decrease.

We advised Mayor Koch that if the situation continued to worsen and there was no other alternative, we would cooperate. We wanted to wait and see. The meeting ended peacefully, with little animosity. Koch's respect for the contract provisions precluded unnecessary arguing. He had the right to request givebacks, but that was as far as he could go. In the following months, the city's economy did improve and the request was not raised again. I was fortunate that Koch and the other mayors I dealt with knew they had to live with and work within the contract.

The Sanctity of Contract in the Business World

Gerry Schoenfeld, head of the Shubert Organization, the theater group, considers himself a tough negotiator. Gerry, a man with a rough exterior but a heart of mush, related to me his negotiations with Al Pacino. In 1980, a representative of Pacino called Gerry to say that Pacino would like to do Richard III on Broadway. Gerry was receptive: "Since Al Pacino is an event and since he would attract young people to Broadway in Shakespeare, I immediately said we were interested."

At a meeting with Pacino and his representative, Gerry noticed "that Al [Pacino] was shifting in his chair and shrugging his shoulder and appearing to be in considerable pain." He related this to a close friend of Pacino, who told him, "Gerry, Al is Richard." Pacino was already playing the part. This delighted Schoenfeld, who believed the negotiations would go smoothly since the actor was already mentally in the role. He was wrong. The play bombed in Philadelphia. It received poor reviews, and Pacino wanted to cancel the scheduled opening in New York.

Pacino's agent called and said, "Gerry, I want you to know Al is not ready." When Gerry replied, "I expect him to go on on Thursday," the night the show was to open, Pacino's agent said, according to Gerry, "Well he's not ready, and you're in trouble." He repeated this statement, and Schoenfeld broke up the conversation.

Sanctity of contract came into play. Schoenfeld made it clear that Pacino would be sued for the cost of the production. The nice guy took off the gloves and went into the fray bare-fisted. He didn't have to use his legal arsenal. Pacino went on. Pacino's lawyer understood sanctity of contract, not to mention the damaging publicity that a lawsuit would cause.

At the opening night party at Sardi's, Gerry Schoenfeld and Pacino literally kissed and made up, as a picture in *People* magazine showed—a fitting way to end a dispute over a contract.

This was an example of how confrontation can be therapeutic. Despite all the sturm und drang, Jerry and Al went on to have a good relationship.

A close friend asked for my help with an employment contract. The terms of the contract were fairly standard, except for one major twist. My friend wanted to use this job as a stepping-stone to bigger and better things. He felt that in a few years, he'd be ready to move on. Knowing this, I questioned why he wanted a five-year contract, which seemed counterproductive. "Why tie yourself down for five years?" I asked. He said he figured he could break the contract because of other factors. I told him I would not help him.

I could not condone his accepting a term of the contract that he had no intention of fulfilling. "Ask for three years," I recommended. Yes, he could have agreed to five years and then tried to amend the contract later, but why play games? He agreed with me.

The lesson here is simple: you don't agree to a contract you are not prepared to live with. I never did, and I didn't want my friend to indulge himself in this fashion.

WHERE THE CONTRACT IS NOT SACROSANCT

When I was in Turkey in 1954, I had an interesting personal experience that for me symbolized the nature of contractual relationships in that country. I had heard from some of the American businessmen there of their difficulty with agreements, whether with the Turkish government or with Turkish businessmen. The Americans would shore up their agreements by adding some mechanism for punishment if the contract was violated.

Our labor relations group in Turkey spent a few months in each of five major cities. We decided to go to one city, Izmir, at the same time the annual fair was taking place. It was very hard trying to get a place to stay, and even more difficult for me because my wife, Sarah, and our two children at that time were going to leave Ankara for a few months to stay with me in Izmir. Finding a good apartment was a real challenge. I had to settle for an apartment that did not meet even my minimal requirements.

The apartment was roomy enough, although cosmetically it was very unattractive. There were broken windows, the paint on the walls was peeling, and so forth. I went into some strong negotiations with the landlord. The negotiations were strong because Turkish businessmen are not lightweights. They drive a tough bargain. However, we did reach an agreement. He would take care of the majority of the cosmetic work and provide us with a refrigerator, which he would rent. I would take care of the remaining repairs and buy a small stove that he could keep after we moved out. The deal seemed appropriate. It was costly to me, but I had to get an apartment. Necessity is a great engine for negotiations.

Things seemed to be going according to plan. He was fixing up the place, and I was becoming rather pleased with it. However, the promised refrigerator was not rented. This appliance was an absolute must for us, especially with two small children. I confronted the landlord.

He made all kinds of excuses. He insisted that it was terribly difficult to get a refrigerator and that it was much too costly. I told him that a deal was a deal. It was imperative that he obtain the refrigerator for me. He then looked at me and said, "Well, I don't know if I can do it." Since we were communicating in French, which I didn't speak well, I wanted to make sure that I was hearing right. I said, "We made an agreement. You said that you were going to obtain the refrigerator. I want that refrigerator." He then replied in open innocence that yes, he made an agreement, but I had to remember that he was a Turk and sometimes agreements weren't carried out.

I was furious, but I had a secret weapon—my wife. I told the landlord that he had better get the refrigerator because he really didn't know what he was in for. He was a little nervous but he still held out.

When Sarah arrived, I told her about the problem. Sarah confronted the landlord. He then knew what I was talking about. She knew some Turkish, and she used it well. She also used it at a high decibel level. The walls began to shake. He looked at me and shook his head in bewilderment. He was defeated. He mumbled an apology and asked me to go with him. We followed him through a labyrinth of streets in a shopping section of Izmir to arrive at a store where they had a usable refrigerator.

The landlord now proceeded to bargain with the owner of the store. He was in pain. I didn't realize it, but obviously renting a refrigerator was no small thing in Turkey. It was costly. But this was no longer my concern. They haggled and I listened. I didn't understand most of what they were saying, but we got the refrigerator. Although the negotiations were ultimately successful, his excuse always stayed with me: "I am a Turk."

In the context of his own culture, this landlord felt strongly that he could violate the contract. This was done all the time and accepted in his culture. He had no doubt that I should have agreed with him and tried to work it out. But this was not the world from which I came. More important, it certainly wasn't the world from which my wife came.

Americans take for granted that a contractual relationship or an agreement is sacrosanct. You would never break an agreement for frivolous reasons or make an agreement that you didn't intend to keep. But as I became more involved in international affairs, I realized that the American style is an exception in many areas of the world. Agreements, contracts, and even laws could be aspirations rather than commitments to be carried out.

In many parts of the world, the law is grandiose. It gives people rights and benefits exceeding those in the United States. However, those laws are meaningless. The constitution in many countries is routinely disregarded and not even binding in court. Labor unions in these countries, when they exist, suffer dramatically, not just from persecution and discrimination, but also from the insecurity of ambiguous and unenforceable law.

The United States refuses to ratify many International Labor Organization conventions. These conventions define collective bargaining rights, rights to organize, and other standards to ensure workers' dignity. On the other hand, many developing countries ratify most of the conventions but never carry them out. Since the ILO has an inadequate punitive mechanism, this practice can continue. The dramatic difference here is the attitude toward law and contract. To Americans, the law is guarantee, not merely an aspiration or goal.

We are a country respectful of the law. We expect to be protected by the law. We even expect dignity from the law. And we believe that our contractual relationships, once agreed on, have the sanctity of law.

Negotiations are a significant part of American life. The binding nature of the contract that we negotiate, whether it is a divorce contract, a business contract, or a collective bargaining agreement between labor and management, gives us security and defines us as a culture. We could not exist as a law-abiding nation or a people of dignity if we did not uphold the sanctity of the contractual relationship.

INDEX

Printed in the United States
By Bookmasters